THEODORE ROOSEVELT

THEODORE ROOSEVELT

Lois Markham

CHELSEA HOUSE PUBLISHERS
NEW YORK

MANAGING EDITOR: William P. Hansen
ASSOCIATE EDITOR: John Haney
CONSULTANT: Mark Sufrin
EDITORIAL STAFF: Linda Cuckovich
　　　　　　　　Susan Quist
　　　　　　　　Katherine Melchior
ART DIRECTOR: Susan Lusk
LAYOUT: Irene Friedman
COVER DESIGN: Peterson Design
PICTURE RESEARCH: Leah Malamed

　5　7　9　8　6　4

Library of Congress Cataloging in Publications Data

Markham, Lois. THEODORE ROOSEVELT.

(World leaders past and present)
Bibliography: p.
Includes index.
Summary: A biography of the twenty-sixth President of the United States.
1. Roosevelt, Theodore, 1858–1919. 2. Presidents—United States—Biography.
3. United States—Politics and government—1901–1909.
4. United States—Politics and government—1909–1913.
[1. Roosevelt, Theodore, 1858–1919. 2. Presidents] I. Title.
E757 M37 1984　　973.91′1′0924 [B] [92] 84-15552

ISBN 0-87754-553-7
　　　　0-7910-0663-8 (pbk.)

Photos courtesy of AP/Wide World Photos
Cover photos courtesy of Culver Pictures, AP/Wide World Photos,
and the United States Department of the Interior

Contents

John Adams
John Quincy Adams
Konrad Adenauer
Alexander the Great
Salvador Allende
Marc Antony
Corazon Aquino
Yasir Arafat
King Arthur
Hafez al-Assad
Kemal Atatürk
Attila
Clement Attlee
Augustus Caesar
Menachem Begin
David Ben-Gurion
Otto von Bismarck
Léon Blum
Simon Bolívar
Cesare Borgia
Willy Brandt
Leonid Brezhnev
Julius Caesar
John Calvin
Jimmy Carter
Fidel Castro
Catherine the Great
Charlemagne
Chiang Kai-Shek
Winston Churchill
Georges Clemenceau
Cleopatra
Constantine the Great
Hernán Cortés
Oliver Cromwell
Georges-Jacques
  Danton
Jefferson Davis
Moshe Dayan
Charles de Gaulle
Eamon De Valera
Eugene Debs
Deng Xiaoping
Benjamin Disraeli
Alexander Dubček
François & Jean-Claude
  Duvalier
Dwight Eisenhower
Eleanor of Aquitaine
Elizabeth I
Faisal
Ferdinand & Isabella
Francisco Franco
Benjamin Franklin

Frederick the Great
Indira Gandhi
Mohandas Gandhi
Giuseppe Garibaldi
Amin & Bashir Gemayel
Genghis Khan
William Gladstone
Mikhail Gorbachev
Ulysses S. Grant
Ernesto "Che" Guevara
Tenzin Gyatso
Alexander Hamilton
Dag Hammarskjöld
Henry VIII
Henry of Navarre
Paul von Hindenburg
Hirohito
Adolf Hitler
Ho Chi Minh
King Hussein
Ivan the Terrible
Andrew Jackson
James I
Wojciech Jaruzelski
Thomas Jefferson
Joan of Arc
Pope John XXIII
Pope John Paul II
Lyndon Johnson
Benito Juárez
John Kennedy
Robert Kennedy
Jomo Kenyatta
Ayatollah Khomeini
Nikita Khrushchev
Kim Il Sung
Martin Luther King, Jr.
Henry Kissinger
Kublai Khan
Lafayette
Robert E. Lee
Vladimir Lenin
Abraham Lincoln
David Lloyd George
Louis XIV
Martin Luther
Judas Maccabeus
James Madison
Nelson & Winnie
  Mandela
Mao Zedong
Ferdinand Marcos
George Marshall

Mary, Queen of Scots
Tomáš Masaryk
Golda Meir
Klemens von Metternich
James Monroe
Hosni Mubarak
Robert Mugabe
Benito Mussolini
Napoléon Bonaparte
Gamal Abdel Nasser
Jawaharlal Nehru
Nero
Nicholas II
Richard Nixon
Kwame Nkrumah
Daniel Ortega
Mohammed Reza Pahlavi
Thomas Paine
Charles Stewart
  Parnell
Pericles
Juan Perón
Peter the Great
Pol Pot
Muammar el-Qaddafi
Ronald Reagan
Cardinal Richelieu
Maximilien Robespierre
Eleanor Roosevelt
Franklin Roosevelt
Theodore Roosevelt
Anwar Sadat
Haile Selassie
Prince Sihanouk
Jan Smuts
Joseph Stalin
Sukarno
Sun Yat-sen
Tamerlane
Mother Teresa
Margaret Thatcher
Josip Broz Tito
Toussaint L'Ouverture
Leon Trotsky
Pierre Trudeau
Harry Truman
Queen Victoria
Lech Walesa
George Washington
Chaim Weizmann
Woodrow Wilson
Xerxes
Emiliano Zapata
Zhou Enlai

CHELSEA HOUSE PUBLISHERS

ON LEADERSHIP
Arthur M. Schlesinger, jr.

LEADERSHIP, it may be said, is really what makes the world go round. Love no doubt smooths the passage; but love is a private transaction between consenting adults. Leadership is a public trans-action with history. The idea of leadership affirms the capacity of individuals to move, inspire and mobilize masses of people so that they act together in pursuit of an end. Sometimes leadership serves good purposes, sometimes bad; but whether the end is benign or evil, great leaders are those men and women who leave their per-sonal stamp on history.

Now, the very concept of leadership implies the proposition that individuals can make a difference. This proposition has never been universally accepted. From classical times to the present day, eminent thinkers have regarded individuals as no more than the agents and pawns of larger forces, whether the gods and goddesses of the ancient world or, in the modern era, race, class, nation, the dialectic, the will of the people, the spirit of the times, history itself. Against such forces, the individual dwindles into insignificance.

So contends the thesis of historical determinism. Tolstoy's great novel *War and Peace* offers a famous statement of the case. Why, Tolstoy asked, did millions of men in the Napoleonic wars, denying their human feelings and their common sense, move back and forth across Europe slaughtering their fellows? "The war," Tolstoy answered, "was bound to happen simply because it was bound to happen." All prior history predetermined it. As for leaders, they, Tolstoy said, "are but the labels that serve to give a name to an end and, like labels, they have the least possible connection with the event." The greater the leader, "the more conspicuous the inevi-tability and the predestination of every act he commits." The leader, said Tolstoy, is "the slave of history."

Determinism takes many forms. Marxism is the determin-ism of class, Nazism the determinism of race. But the idea of men and women as the slaves of history runs athwart the deepest hu-man instincts. Rigid determinism abolishes the idea of human freedom—the assumption of free choice that underlies every move we make, every word we speak, every thought we think. It abolishes the idea of human responsibility, since it is manifestly unfair to reward or punish people for actions that are by definition beyond their control. No one can live consistently by any deterministic creed. The Marxist states prove this themselves by their extreme susceptibility to the cult of leadership.

More than that, history refutes the idea that individuals make no difference. In December 1931 a British politician crossing Park Avenue in New York City between 76th and 77th Streets around ten-thirty at night looked in the wrong direction and was knocked down by an automobile—a moment, he later recalled, of a man aghast, a world aglare: "I do not understand why I was not broken like an eggshell or squashed like a gooseberry." Fourteen months later an American politician, sitting in an open car in Miami, Florida, was fired on by an assassin; the man beside him was hit. Those who believe that individuals make no difference to history might well ponder whether the next two decades would have been the same had Mario Contasini's car killed Winston Churchill in 1931 and Giuseppe Zangara's bullet killed Franklin Roosevelt in 1933. Suppose, in addition, that Adolf Hitler had been killed in the street fighting during the Munich *Putsch* of 1923 and that Lenin had died of typhus during the First World War. What would the 20th century be like now?

For better or for worse, individuals do make a difference. "The notion that a people can run itself and its affairs anonymously," wrote the philosopher William James, "is now well known to be the silliest of absurdities. Mankind does nothing save through initiatives on the part of inventors, great or small, and imitation by the rest of us—these are the sole factors in human progress. Individuals of genius show the way, and set the patterns, which common people then adopt and follow."

Leadership, James suggests, means leadership in thought as well as in action. In the long run, leaders in thought may well make the greater difference to the world. But, as Woodrow Wilson once said, "Those only are leaders of men, in the general eye, who lead in action. . . . It is at their hands that new thought gets its translation into the crude language of deeds." Leaders in thought often invent in solitude and obscurity, leaving to later generations the tasks of imitation. Leaders in action—the leaders portrayed in this series— have to be effective in their own time.

And they cannot be effective by themselves. They must act in response to the rhythms of their age. Their genius must be adapted, in a phrase of William James's, "to the receptivities of the moment." Leaders are useless without followers. "There goes the mob," said the French politician hearing a clamor in the streets. "I am their leader. I must follow them." Great leaders turn the inchoate emotions of the mob to purposes of their own. They seize on the opportunities of their time, the hopes, fears, frustrations, crises, potentialities.

They succeed when events have prepared the way for them, when the community is waiting to be aroused, when they can provide the clarifying and organizing ideas. Leadership ignites the circuit between the individual and the mass and thereby alters history.

It may alter history for better or for worse. Leaders have been responsible for the most extravagant follies and most monstrous crimes that have beset suffering humanity. They have also been vital in such gains as humanity has made in individual freedom, religious and racial tolerance, social justice and respect for human rights.

There is no sure way to tell in advance who is going to lead for good and who for evil. But a glance at the gallery of men and women in *World Leaders—Past and Present* suggests some useful tests.

One test is this: do leaders lead by force or by persuasion? By command or by consent? Through most of history leadership was exercised by the divine right of authority. The duty of followers was to defer and to obey. "Theirs not to reason why,/ Theirs but to do and die." On occasion, as with the so-called "enlightened despots" of the 18th century in Europe, absolutist leadership was animated by humane purposes. More often, absolutism nourished the passion for domination, land, gold and conquest and resulted in tyranny.

The great revolution of modern times has been the revolution of equality. The idea that all people should be equal in their legal condition has undermined the old structures of authority, hierarchy and deference. The revolution of equality has had two contrary effects on the nature of leadership. For equality, as Alexis de Tocqueville pointed out in his great study *Democracy in America*, might mean equality in servitude as well as equality in freedom.

"I know of only two methods of establishing equality in the political world," Tocqueville wrote. "Rights must be given to every citizen, or none at all to anyone . . . save one, who is the master of all." There was no middle ground "between the sovereignty of all and the absolute power of one man." In his astonishing prediction of 20th-century totalitarian dictatorship, Tocqueville explained how the revolution of equality could lead to the "*Führerprinzip*" and more terrible absolutism than the world had ever known.

But when rights are given to every citizen and the sovereignty of all is established, the problem of leadership takes a new form, becomes more exacting than ever before. It is easy to issue commands and enforce them by the rope and the stake, the concentration camp and the *gulag*. It is much harder to use argument and achievement to overcome opposition and win consent. The Founding Fathers of the United States understood the difficulty. They believed that history had given them the opportunity to decide, as

Alexander Hamilton wrote in the first Federalist Paper, whether men are indeed capable of basing government on "reflection and choice, or whether they are forever destined to depend . . . on accident and force."

Government by reflection and choice called for a new style of leadership and a new quality of followership. It required leaders to be responsive to popular concerns, and it required followers to be active and informed participants in the process. Democracy does not eliminate emotion from politics; sometimes it fosters demagoguery; but it is confident that, as the greatest of democratic leaders put it, you cannot fool all of the people all of the time. It measures leadership by results and retires those who overreach or falter or fail.

It is true that in the long run despots are measured by results too. But they can postpone the day of judgment, sometimes indefinitely, and in the meantime they can do infinite harm. It is also true that democracy is no guarantee of virtue and intelligence in government, for the voice of the people is not necessarily the voice of God. But democracy, by assuring the rights of opposition, offers built-in resistance to the evils inherent in absolutism. As the theologian Reinhold Niebuhr summed it up, "Man's capacity for justice makes democracy possible, but man's inclination to injustice makes democracy necessary."

A second test for leadership is the end for which power is sought. When leaders have as their goal the supremacy of a master race or the promotion of totalitarian revolution or the acquisition and exploitation of colonies or the protection of greed and privilege or the preservation of personal power, it is likely that their leadership will do little to advance the cause of humanity. When their goal is the abolition of slavery, the liberation of women, the enlargement of opportunity for the poor and powerless, the extension of equal rights to racial minorities, the defense of the freedoms of expression and opposition, it is likely that their leadership will increase the sum of human liberty and welfare.

Leaders have done great harm to the world. They have also conferred great benefits. You will find both sorts in this series. Even "good" leaders must be regarded with a certain wariness. Leaders are not demigods; they put on their trousers one leg after another just like ordinary mortals. No leader is infallible, and every leader needs to be reminded of this at regular intervals. Irreverence irritates leaders but is their salvation. Unquestioning submission corrupts leaders and demeans followers. Making a cult of a leader is always a mistake. Fortunately hero worship generates its own antidote. "Every hero," said Emerson, "becomes a bore at last."

The signal benefit the great leaders confer is to embolden the rest of us to live according to our own best selves, to be active, insistent, and resolute in affirming our own sense of things. For great leaders attest to the reality of human freedom against the supposed inevitabilities of history. And they attest to the wisdom and power that may lie within the most unlikely of us, which is why Abraham Lincoln remains the supreme example of great leadership. A great leader, said Emerson, exhibits new possibilities to all humanity. "We feed on genius. . . . Great men exist that there may be greater men."

Great leaders, in short, justify themselves by emancipating and empowering their followers. So humanity struggles to master its destiny, remembering with Alexis de Tocqueville: "It is true that around every man a fatal circle is traced beyond which he cannot pass; but within the wide verge of that circle he is powerful and free; as it is with man, so with communities."

—*New York*

1

A Frail and Nervous Child

July 1, 1898. By noon the temperature near Santiago, Cuba, had risen to 100 degrees. Colonel Theodore Roosevelt of the First Volunteer Cavalry, known as the Rough Riders, was impatiently awaiting orders. He and his men had been huddled at the base of a small hill for an hour and a half. Spanish forces holding the hill kept up a constant, deadly gunfire.

Colonel Roosevelt was not used to waiting. Nor was he accustomed to taking orders. In fact, he had been strongly tempted to charge up the hill before receiving instructions from the general. Finally the orders came. Roosevelt leaped to his horse (only senior officers had horses) and began the assault on Kettle Hill. It was the moment he had been dreaming of all his life.

Bullets rained down from the top of the hill. One ripped through a Rough Rider in front of him. Through glasses fogged with sweat the Colonel noticed that some of his men were hesitating. He shouted at the terrified soldiers, "Are you afraid to stand up when I am on horseback?"

At one point a bullet grazed his elbow. At last he neared the top of the hill. Spanish soldiers were

Theodore Roosevelt, seen here in Cuba in 1898, thought himself superior to the regular army officers, although experts now consider that his famous charge at Kettle Hill on July 1, 1898 was foolhardy.

Theodore Roosevelt at age 10. Despite poor health, Theodore was an energetic and happy child.

fleeing before him. With a revolver he fired at one of them. The man fell, "neatly as a jackrabbit." A few minutes later, the Rough Riders took Kettle Hill.

It was a moment of supreme glory for Theodore Roosevelt. In the thick of battle, without a thought for his own safety, he had proven a courageous and inspiring leader. It was the realization of his life's dream to be a hero. And it was the reward for a solemn promise made to his father 28 years earlier.

"I will make my body," young Theodore had sworn. He was 12 years old at the time, a sickly, undersized child. One day his father called him into his study for a serious talk.

"Theodore," he said in his kindly but firm manner, "you have the mind but you have not the body, and without the help of the body the mind cannot go as far as it should. You must make your body."

It was at that moment that young Theodore took his vow. Then, with grit and determination, he proceeded to keep it. For years he lifted weights, swung at punching bags, boxed, rowed, and swam. Finally, long after his father's death, he achieved the physical strength to match his enormously energetic mind.

It was a mind that often seemed to take him in several directions at once, some of them quite contradictory. He was a man of action, yet he enjoyed the quiet pleasure of reading two or three books a day. He was an Eastern aristocrat who spent two happy years as a rancher in the Wild West. He glorified the warrior spirit, but he was also a devoted family man. He was a careful student of nature and a pioneering conservationist, but he was also an enthusiastic big game hunter. A firm believer in democracy, he nevertheless felt that more "advanced" nations had a responsibility to dominate those he considered "backward."

Roosevelt's internal contradictions inspired vastly

Colonel Theodore Roosevelt and troops of the First Volunteer Cavalry (known as the Rough Riders) in Cuba in 1898, during the Spanish-American War.

differing opinions of him. American writer Mark Twain once called him "clearly insane." King Edward VII of England considered him the "greatest moral force of the age." Perhaps his friend Sir Cecil Spring-Rice had the secret behind the contradictions when he said, "You must always remember that the President is about six years old." For it was Roosevelt's eternally youthful enthusiasm for life that dominated his personality.

Theodore Roosevelt, called Teedie as a boy, was born on October 27, 1858, into a prosperous old New York City family. His father's Dutch ancestors had arrived in the New World in 1644. The family's economic standing had steadily improved, and by 1858 the Roosevelts, successful glass importers, were one of New York's leading families.

Teedie's father, also named Theodore, was a kindly, generous, and sociable man. He had little interest in the family business, which he left to his father and brothers while he pursued civic and charitable activities. He was a founder of the Metropolitan Museum of Art and the American Museum of Natural History, as well as the Children's Aid Society, which helped New York City's homeless children.

Theodore senior provided more than money to his charities. He also gave generously of his time and energy. Among other activities, he spent every Sunday evening visiting the Newsboys' Lodging House, where homeless boys could get a clean bed in a warm room for five cents a night. Taking personal interest in the boys, he listened to their stories and offered advice and sympathy.

From his father young Theodore learned a sense of responsibility to people less fortunate than himself. It came from a heartfelt desire to do good, but also from an awareness of his favored position in life.

Teedie's mother was Martha Bullock Roosevelt, nicknamed Mittie. Born in Georgia, she was an attractive and charming woman but had considerably less energy and public spirit than her husband. Her interest was in her home and family. She lavished attention and affection on her children.

Roosevelt in cowboy dress. Crushed by the deaths of his first wife and his mother in February 1884, Roosevelt spent much of the next two years running the ranches he had purchased out west in 1883.

Teedie had an older sister, Anna, called Bamie. A younger brother, Elliott, was born in 1860, and a sister, Corinne, completed the family in 1861. The four children were devoted to both parents, and their home was a loving and lively place, frequently filled with relatives and friends.

In 1861 the Civil War began, causing much soul-searching in the Roosevelt household, where loyalties were divided. Mittie's two brothers were fighting on the side of the Confederacy. Her mother and sister were living with the Roosevelts in New York. During the war, the three women would often pack supplies to be sent to the Confederates.

Theodore senior had a strong sense of duty to his country and favored the Union cause, but he was reluctant to join the Union Army and perhaps someday find himself shooting at his brothers-in-law.

For this reason he made a choice that was open

to wealthy men at the time. He paid for a substitute to take his place in the army. But he did want to serve his country in some capacity, so he invented a volunteer civilian job that kept him traveling to army camps for most of the war. His daughter Corinne later claimed that Teedie had been disturbed by his father's unwillingness to fight in the Civil War. Many have even wondered if Theodore junior later sought military glory to compensate for his father's decision. In any case, there was no question about Teedie's loyalties. Listening to his evening prayers one night, his Aunt Anna heard him ask the Almighty to "grind the Southern troops to powder."

Britain's King Edward VII, with his grandchildren in 1902. He once called Roosevelt "the greatest moral force of the age."

The Metropolitan Museum of Art in New York. Theodore Roosevelt's father was one of the founders of this famous institution.

No doubt the whole family was glad when the war ended in 1865, easing tensions in the household. Mittie was certainly happy to have her husband back home to help discipline their lively children, who were an active group in spite of poor health. Bamie endured almost constant pain from severe curvature of the spine. Corinne had occasional attacks of asthma. Mittie herself had headaches and stomach trouble.

Teedie's health was undoubtedly the worst in the family. In particular, he suffered from nervousness, a weak stomach, and violent attacks of asthma. During an attack he would wheeze and gasp for breath while his distressed parents did whatever they could to help. One popular treatment of the day was to drink strong black coffee. Another was to have the victim smoke vile-smelling cigars.

Union army artillerymen prepare to repel an attack during the American Civil War. Theodore Roosevelt retained his hostility to the Confederate cause for the rest of his life, though he disguised the fact when making political visits to the Southern states.

Some nights his father would bundle Teedie into a horse-drawn carriage and drive him through the city at top speed to force air into his lungs. Often his father took him to the country for a few days, hoping that clean air would help the poor child breathe more easily.

Despite bad health and a frail body, Teedie had a happy childhood. Forced to find quiet entertainment, he discovered the library at an early age and became an avid reader. He especially enjoyed tales of real and imaginary heroes. He later wrote: "I was nervous and timid. . . . I felt a great admiration for men who were fearless and could hold their own in the world, and I had a great desire to be like them."

Theodore was also fascinated by stories about animals, and he developed a consuming interest in natural history and science. He later recalled a striking incident that happened when he was only seven years old:

"I was walking up Broadway, and . . . suddenly saw a dead seal laid out on a slab of wood. That

seal filled me with every possible feeling of romance and adventure. I asked where it was killed, and was informed in the harbor. . . . As long as that seal remained there I haunted the neighborhood of the market day after day. I measured it, and I recall that, not having a tape measure, I had to do my best to get its girth with a folding pocket foot-rule, a difficult undertaking. I carefully made a record of the utterly useless measurements, and at once began to write a natural history of my own, on the strength of that seal. . . . I had vague aspirations of in some way or another owning that seal, but they never got beyond the purely formless stage. I think, however, I did get the seal's skull, and with two of my cousins promptly started what we ambitiously called the 'Roosevelt Museum of Natural History.' ''

Jefferson Davis shortly before his inauguration as president of the Confederate States of America in 1861. Roosevelt later exchanged letters with this former Confederate leader, to whom he once referred as an "unhung traitor."

The "museum" was a reality for a number of years, despite the complaints of family members and servants. They sometimes found it upsetting to live in a household where they might discover a litter of field mice in the ice chest, a snapping turtle tied to the leg of the sink, or a snake in a water pitcher.

Teedie was a serious young scientist, interested not only in collecting and dissecting specimens but also in recording his observations for posterity. Thus, at the age of nine, he wrote a "Natural History of Insects," a well-organized and careful treatment of the topic.

In 1869, when Teedie was eleven, Mittie and Theodore senior planned a year-long grand tour of Europe. They hoped it would improve the health of the whole family, as well as provide an educational experience for the children. A high point of the trip was visiting Mittie's two brothers, who had been living in England since the end of the Civil War. In spite of Teedie's loyalty to the Union cause, he loved his uncles dearly. They were the romantic heroes from his books come to life. They were the fearless men of action he so admired and wanted to imitate.

During the year abroad Teedie wrote in a journal every day, keeping a record of all the things he saw and did. Theodore senior was not a man to waste time. He kept the family busy on sightseeing outings and vigorous hikes through the countryside. Teedie took part in these strenuous activities and enjoyed himself immensely, even though he had severe asthma attacks on several occasions.

When the family returned to New York in May 1870, Theodore senior decided it was time to do something about his oldest son's poor physical condition. The trip, as fun-filled and exciting as it was, had not had any positive effect on Teedie's health. In addition to the asthma, Teedie was still undersized and weak. It was at this point that Theodore senior talked to his son about "making his body" and encouraged him to begin daily workouts at a gymnasium.

Determination in the face of great difficulty was

Had he come to the prize ring, instead of the political arena, it is my conviction he would have been successful. The man is a born fighter.

—MIKE DONOVAN
Roosevelt's boxing teacher

always a characteristic of the future president, and he approached his body-building program with complete dedication. He made progress, but it was very slow.

Just how far he had to go became clear to Teedie once when he was traveling alone to Maine for relief from his asthma. On a stagecoach he encountered two boys his own age. When they began to tease him, Teedie fought back. He was humiliated to discover that either of the boys could easily deflect his blows.

Meanwhile, his interest in natural history grew and his activities expanded. After one summer vacation in New York State's Adirondack Mountains, he made an official contribution to the American Museum of Natural History: one bat, twelve mice, a turtle, the skull of a red squirrel, and four birds' eggs.

His father, always supportive of worthwhile activities, arranged for Teedie to take lessons in taxidermy (the art of stuffing and mounting animal skins). This quickly became Teedie's major passion. His activity, however, was limited by the number of dead animals he could find. To remedy the situation, his father gave him a gun.

Teedie immediately took to the woods near their summer home but found that he was unable to hit anything. It turned out that he had a serious vision problem, one he had probably had all his young life. Soon he was wearing glasses and gazing in wonder at the wider world now opened to him, especially the world of birds.

Glasses, gun, and taxidermy kit went along with Teedie on his famiy's next trip abroad. In October 1872, when he was 14, the family left for another grand tour. For two months they drifted up and down Egypt's Nile River on a houseboat.

Mornings Teedie roamed the shores of the Nile, shooting birds. Then he returned to the houseboat and went to work with his taxidermy kit. By the end of the Nile trip he had shot and stuffed nearly 200 birds. Today such large-scale slaughter would be condemned, but at the time it was standard procedure for naturalists. Even the great artist John

Martha Roosevelt, Theodore's mother, as portrayed by the artist Jennie S. Loos in an 1874 painting.

The capacity to be bored, whether treated as a sin or a misfortune, is an awful handicap.
—THEODORE ROOSEVELT

23

James Audubon killed birds to obtain specimens for painting.

After leaving the Nile, the Roosevelt family traveled through Palestine, Syria, Turkey, Greece, and Austria. Then Teedie, Elliott, and Corinne went to Dresden to live with a German family for the summer. There they took lessons in German and math.

At first the family was taken aback by Teedie's scientific pursuits. He reported that the arsenic he used in taxidermy was taken away and his mice thrown out the window. By the time Teedie left Dresden, however, the family had grown to respect him. The mother said to Mittie, "He will surely one day be a great professor, or who knows, he may become even President of the United States." She may have been the first to recognize the young man's potential for greatness.

By the time he returned home in October 1873, Theodore knew that he wanted to go to Harvard University to pursue a career in science. He started to prepare seriously for college. Except for one brief period, his health had never permitted him to go to school. Even now he continued to study at home with tutors. But he worked extremely hard, and in September 1876 he set off for Cambridge, Massa-

In contrast to the happiness of Theodore's childhood, other children of his generation suffered severe exploitation throughout the 19th century. Greatly concerned with the plight of American labor during his career, Roosevelt contributed a number of essays to reports published by the National Child Labor Committee.

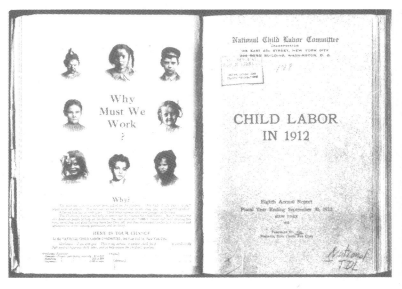

24

Roosevelt at Harvard. Active both socially and intellectually during his four years there, he was not particularly popular, probably because he was more energetic than was fashionable among Harvard undergraduates at the time.

chusetts, to begin his life at Harvard. It was a big step for a young man who had never been far from the warm, loving family that had always treated him so specially.

But he was ready for new challenges. At first he was considered rather odd by his Harvard classmates, but eventually most came to respect and like him for the same qualities that won him friends throughout his life—his energy, enthusiasm, honesty, and strength of character.

In college Theodore's asthma improved significantly, but in spite of constant effort he still looked like a weakling. One classmate, watching him work out in the gym, described him as a "youth in the kindergarten stage of physical development." That same classmate later went ice-skating with Theodore on a frigid New England day with the wind blowing at gale speeds. After three hours of vigorous activity he had a new respect for young Roosevelt's endurance.

Stand the gaff, play fair; be a good man to camp out with.
—THEODORE ROOSEVELT

Henry Cabot Lodge, whose history classes at Harvard Theodore studiously avoided due to their intellectual severity. Lodge eventually became a leading Republican and one of Roosevelt's principal political supporters and allies.

Two very important things happened during Theodore's years at Harvard. First, in February 1878, when he was 19, his beloved father died at the age of 46. Without a doubt, his father had been the guiding light of Theodore's life, and he grieved deeply. Years later his sister Corinne wrote that Theodore had told her he never made any serious decision as president without considering what his father's position would have been.

The second event was a happy one. In his third year at Harvard, Theodore met and immediately fell in love with Alice Hathaway Lee, a lovely young lady from a prominent Boston family. He said later that

Theodore Roosevelt (at left) with his brother Elliott in 1879. Roosevelt was at Harvard at this time, and already courting the young woman who would become his first wife, Alice Hathaway Lee.

Theodore Roosevelt always believed in the importance of childhood in character-building, and took great interest in youth organizations such as the Boy Scouts of America.

he had made up his mind to marry her the day they met. It took a bit longer to convince Alice and her family.

During his final two years at Harvard, Roosevelt was extremely active. He worked hard at his studies, had a wide circle of friends and a busy social life, pursued his athletic interests (boxing, fencing, football), and courted Alice extravagantly. In June 1880 he graduated from Harvard, and in October he and Alice were married.

Young Teedie, the frail asthmatic boy with the odor of formaldehyde clinging to him, had become a man. He was now the head of a household that included a mother, two sisters, a younger brother, and a new wife. Where would he go from here?

Homage to Theodore Roosevelt—as expressed by the National Council of the Boy Scouts of America in a resolution drafted in 1919.

THEODORE ROOSEVELT

Resolution drafted by Hermann Hagedorn and adopted by the National Council of the Boy Scouts of America at their annual meeting, 1919.

HE was found faithful over a few things and he was made ruler over many; he cut his own trail clean and straight and millions followed him toward the light.

He was frail; he made himself a tower of strength. He was timid; he made himself a lion of courage. He was a dreamer; he became one of the great doers of all time.

Men put their trust in him; women found a champion in him; kings stood in awe of him, but children made him their playmate.

He broke a nation's slumber with his cry, and it rose up. He touched the eyes of blind men with a flame and gave them vision. Souls became swords through him; swords became servants of God.

He was loyal to his country, and he exacted loyalty; he loved many lands, but he loved his own land best.

He was terrible in battle, but tender to the weak; joyous and tireless, being free from self-pity; clean with a cleanness that cleansed the air like a gale.

His courtesy knew no wealth or class; his friendship, no creed or color or race. His courage stood every onslaught of savage beast and ruthless man, of loneliness, of victory, of defeat. His mind was eager, his heart was true, his body and spirit defiant of obstacles, ready to meet what might come.

He fought injustice and tyranny; bore sorrow gallantly; loved all nature, bleak spaces and hardy companions, hazardous adventure and the zest of battle. Wherever he went he carried his own pack, and in the uttermost parts of the earth he kept his conscience for his guide.

2

A Man You Can't Frighten

As he turned 22, Theodore Roosevelt's life lay before him like a blank book. He sincerely wanted to write glorious, heroic scenes on the pages of that book. But he knew not what the content of those scenes would be. For reasons never wholly explained, he had discarded the idea of being a scientist. For the next 20 years, he drifted from one calling to another, never quite sure where he was headed.

In the fall of 1880, however, Theodore Roosevelt was first and foremost a happy newlywed. After the wedding he brought Alice to New York to live with his mother, sisters, and brother. The young couple soon became very active socially. Almost every night saw them at some cultural or social affair: receptions, dinners, theater, opera, private balls. Often they went from one event to another, arriving home in the early hours of the morning.

Late-night partying did not mean that Theodore spent his days resting. After deciding against science as a career, he enrolled in the Columbia University law school. On a typical day Roosevelt was up by 7:45 A.M., ready for the three-mile walk to

A replica of Theodore Roosevelt's ranch cabin in western Dakota where he retreated for two years following the death of his first wife in February 1884, only returning to the East to visit his daughter.

Theodore Roosevelt in 1885. He believed so strongly in the benefits of life outdoors that he tended to brag about his pioneering accomplishments. For the youth of his day he suggested "a short course of riding bucking ponies," among other pursuits.

THE

NAVAL WAR OF 1812

OR THE

HISTORY OF THE UNITED STATES NAVY
DURING THE LAST WAR WITH
GREAT BRITAIN

BY

THEODORE ROOSEVELT

NEW YORK
G. P. PUTNAM'S SONS
27 & 29 WEST 23D STREET
1882

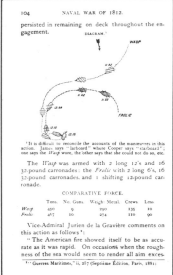

104   NAVAL WAR OF 1812.

persisted in remaining on deck throughout the engagement.

DIAGRAM.

WASP

FROLIC

'It is difficult to reconcile the accounts of the manœuvres in this action. James says "larboard" where Cooper says "starboard"; one says the *Wasp* wore, the other says that she could not do so, etc.

The *Wasp* was armed with 2 long 12's and 16 32-pound carronades; the *Frolic* with 2 long 6's, 16 32-pound carronades, and 1 shifting 12-pound carronade.

COMPARATIVE FORCE.

	Tons.	No. Guns.	Weight Metal.	Crews	Loss
Wasp	450	9	250	135	10
Frolic	467	10	274	110	90

Vice-Admiral Jurien de la Gravière comments on this action as follows[1]:

" The American fire showed itself to be as accurate as it was rapid. On occasions when the roughness of the sea would seem to render all aim exces-

[1] "Guerres Maritimes," ii, 287 (Septième Édition, Paris, 1881)

An extract from Roosevelt's book *The Naval War of 1812*, published in New York in 1882. British critics considered Roosevelt's book so outstanding that he was invited to contribute an essay to a major British reference work devoted to naval history.

campus. When classes ended, he dashed off to the library to work on a scholarly book he had begun in college, *The Naval War of 1812*. At 3:00 P.M. he returned home to take Alice or his mother for a ride around New York City. By then it was time to dress for dinner and the evening's social engagements.

Despite his hectic schedule, Theodore still found time to frequent the local Republican Club. During this period politics was not an approved activity for socially prominent young men. But Theodore Roosevelt was not a typical wealthy young man. His father had instilled in him a sense of social responsibility. Although his father's charitable and civic activities did not appeal to him, he was interested in improving life in New York City through politics.

At first young Roosevelt was ignored by the regulars at the Republican Club. They were, for the most part, people far below him socially. They probably wondered what this dandy was doing in their midst, but eventually his outspoken honesty won their respect. Some even talked of making him a candidate for public office. It was not idle chatter.

In 1881, having quit law school, Theodore was elected to the first of three one-year terms in the New York State legislature. It meant he had to spend most of the week in Albany away from his family, and he sorely missed Alice. But politics was now his calling, and he would do what he must to follow it.

Fellow legislators at first regarded Roosevelt as a harmless oddball. But, just as in college, once people got to know him, they came to like and admire him. They might disagree with him, but they could not ignore him.

During his three years in the legislature Theodore become known for his stands against corruption in government. But perhaps the most significant event for his future political development was his introduction to the reality of poverty in New York City.

The cigar-makers union had introduced a bill to outlaw the making of cigars in workers' homes.

Entire families were living and producing cigars in tiny, overcrowded, unhealthy apartments. The owners of cigar-making firms opposed the bill, since it would cost them much more money to provide factories for their workers.

Samuel Gompers, head of the union, invited Theodore to visit the tenements where the cigar-makers lived and worked, to dramatize the need for legislation. Nothing in his past had prepared him for the poverty and squalor he saw there.

Originally Roosevelt had planned to vote against the bill, believing that businessmen had a right to conduct their affairs as they pleased. But Theodore Roosevelt was not a moral coward. Though he had strong convictions, he was not afraid to change his mind when presented with good reasons. He voted for the cigar-makers' bill. More important, he never forgot the tenement scenes.

In 1884 Theodore Roosevelt's life was going very well indeed. He had just begun his third term in the legislature. He had won reelection with a large majority, and his political star was rising. In addition, his beloved Alice was pregnant. Then tragedy struck.

On February 13, 1884, Theodore received a telegram in Albany saying that Alice had given birth to a healthy baby girl the night before. He immediately left for New York to welcome the new arrival. At his front door he was met by his brother Elliott, who cried, "There is a curse on this house! Mother is dying and Alice is dying too."

Mittie had been sick with what was believed to be a cold. It was actually typhoid fever. Alice, after a normal childbirth, was dying of Bright's disease, an inflammation of the kidneys. By 3:00 A.M. on February 14, Mittie was dead; at 2:00 P.M. the same day Alice died.

That night Theodore wrote in his diary, "The light has gone out of my life." Several months later he wrote a brief memorial to Alice. He never spoke of her again, not even to their daughter, who had been given her mother's name.

Leaving the infant Alice with his sister Bamie, Theodore finished out the legislative season in

American labor leader Samuel Gompers, who headed the cigar-makers union in 1884 when Roosevelt supported his bill abolishing cigar manufacturing at home.

Shown here are the three brands which Roosevelt used to identify the cattle on his ranches in the Dakotas. Although the hard winter of 1886–7 killed 65% of his stock, Roosevelt thought little of the financial loss, considering the profits of experience more valuable than money.

CHIMNEY BUTTE RANCH.
THEODORE ROOSEVELT, Proprietor.
FERRIS & MERRIFIELD, Managers.

P. O. address, Little Missouri, D. T. Range, Little Missouri, 8 miles south of railroad.

as in cut on left hip and right side, both or either, and down cut dewlap. Horse brand, on left hip.

ELKHORN RANCH.
THEODORE ROOSEVELT, Proprietor.
SEAWALL & DOW, Managers.

P. O. address, Little Missouri, D. T. Range, Little Missouri, twenty-five miles north of railroad.

as in cut, on left side, on right, or the reverse. Horse brand, on right or left shoulder.

Albany. He then headed west to the Dakota Badlands in search of solitude and time for reflection. He had planned his whole future based on a life with Alice. Without her he felt like a tumbleweed, ungrounded. For the present he would take comfort in hard physical labor and the wonders of nature.

He had been to the Dakota Territory earlier. In fact, on a hunting trip a few years back, he had shot one of the region's few remaining buffaloes. Now he purchased several thousand head of cattle, built two ranches (in what is now North Dakota), and began a career raising cattle. He was not alone. Many other ranchers and cowboys had recently settled there, attracted by the cheap land and rugged life.

At first Roosevelt struck the rough-and-ready cowboys as a strange dude. Not only was he short and slight, but he wore glasses! Behind his back, they called him Old Four-Eyes. But they soon learned that the Eastern aristocrat could be as tough as they were. In a saloon one night, a gun-slinging cowboy made fun of Theodore's glasses. With one punch, Theodore knocked him out cold.

Theodore Roosevelt and ranch-hand William Sewall (at left) in 1884. The two men first met in 1876 when Sewall acted as guide to Roosevelt's party during a walking holiday in Maine.

Although he never learned to ride or rope very well, Theodore did both with his usual enthusiasm. He also earned the respect of the ranch hands by riding in cattle roundups. Once, he was in the saddle for 40 hours straight, wore out 5 horses, and survived a terrifying stampede.

Life on the cattle range was a far cry from the polite society of New York City. One day Theodore realized that a boat he kept on a nearby river had been stolen. He believed that ignoring the theft would encourage future lawlessness, so he set out after the thieves with two of his men.

For three days they traveled the river in a makeshift boat. The temperature dropped below zero at times, but the determined Roosevelt caught up with the outlaws. It took another six days to make the return trip because of ice jams on the river. Also, they had to guard the prisoners day and night, since it was too cold to put handcuffs on them.

When Theodore finally brought the men to justice, he was told that anyone else would have shot them without hesitation or fear of punishment. But that was not Theodore Roosevelt's way. To him living by the law was of great importance, and rules were not made to be broken.

One of his rules was not to waste time. During his six days on the river with the thieves, Theodore managed to read the Russian novel *Anna Karenina*! As much as he relished the rugged life of the range, he maintained his love for books and the challenge of new ideas. In fact, while in Dakota, Roosevelt decided that writing would be his life's career. He was already at work on *Hunting Trips of a Ranchman.* He also drew on his Western experiences for several later books.

During his three years in the Dakota Territory, Theodore made several trips back East. On one of these visits he renewed his acquaintance with Edith Carow, a friend of the family since childhood. In fact, before Theodore went off to Harvard and met Alice, it was assumed that they might someday be married. Now Theodore and Edith became secretly engaged.

Theodore suffered acute pangs of guilt for being

> *There are no words that can tell the hidden spirit of the wilderness, that can reveal its mystery, its melancholy, and its charm. There is delight in the hardy life of the open, in long rides rifle in hand, in the thrill of the fight with dangerous game.*
> —THEODORE ROOSEVELT

Theodore Roosevelt in 1886, when he was the Republican candidate for mayor of New York, running against an independent Democrat, and socialist writer Henry George.

unfaithful to Alice. At the time, it was not uncommon for a widower to remain unmarried for the rest of his life out of respect for his dead wife. But Theodore knew that he was a man who needed a family to give him roots.

His feelings for Alice had been the total infatuation of a first romance. She was beautiful and charming but lacked a strong personality. Friends later speculated that Alice would never have grown into the forceful, well-rounded woman that Theodore Roosevelt needed as a lifetime companion.

An artist's impression of events in Chicago in early 1886. Workers rioted in protest against police brutality following the death of a policeman in an anarchist bombing. The increasing confrontation between workers and employers in America's rapidly expanding industrial areas was a major issue in the New York mayoral elections later that same year.

Edith Carow was just such a woman—strong, self-contained, calm, practical, and deeply in love with the explosive Theodore. Their relationship was based on the genuine affection and respect that develops best over a long period of time.

By October 1886 cattle-ranching in the Dakotas was looking less and less promising. There had been a severe drought, and an extremely bitter winter destroyed two-thirds of Roosevelt's cattle. Well-organized cattle thieves plagued the region. Roosevelt's ranches were losing money, and his inheritance was dwindling. As a result, he entrusted

ILLINOIS—THE ANARCHIST-LABOR TROUBLES IN CHICAGO—A POLICE PATROL-WAGON ATTACKED BY A MOB OF 12,000 RIOTERS, MAY 3d.
FROM SKETCHES BY C. BUNNELL AND CHARLES UPHAM.—SEE PAGE 174.

his ranches to his foremen and returned to New York permanently.

Although Roosevelt did not gain financially from his time in the Dakotas, there were physical, spiritual, and perhaps even political rewards. At last he was a sturdy, rugged physical specimen, someone who could take care of himself under the toughest circumstances. And he felt a kinship with Western settlers that was unique in an Eastern politician.

Back in New York City, he was persuaded to run for mayor on the Republican ticket. He expected to lose and did. Shortly after the election he and his sister Bamie sailed for England, where he was reunited with Edith. They were married in London on December 6, 1886.

After a European honeymoon, the couple returned to the United States and moved into a new 22-room house on Sagamore Hill in Oyster Bay, Long Island. Theodore had started construction on it before Alice died. For the rest of their lives, no matter where else Edith and Theodore lived, Sagamore Hill was their real home, the oasis to which they returned for rest and relaxation. There they entertained friends, enjoyed the country life, and began their own family.

Theodore junior was born in 1887, Kermit in 1889, Ethel in 1891, Archibald in 1894, and Quentin in 1897. With his daughter Alice they were the joy of Theodore's life. They enabled him to free the child in himself, to express the boyish enthusiasm that was always a central part of his character.

By 1887 the cattle ranches had failed completely. Theodore supplemented what was left of his inheritance by writing at Sagamore Hill. He began working on *The Winning of the West*, which became his most notable book. He believed he was out of politics for good, but politics was in Theodore Roosevelt's blood. Furthermore, he never lost his sense of duty to his country. When Republican President Benjamin Harrison took office in 1889, Theodore admitted to his friend Henry Cabot Lodge, a Massachusetts congressman, that he would like to reenter the political arena.

The only trouble I ever had with managing him was that... he wanted to put an end to all the evil in the world between sunrise and sunset.
—BENJAMIN HARRISON

Benjamin Harrison, president of the United States from 1889 to 1893. Throughout 1888 Roosevelt campaigned vigorously for Harrison, whom he thought able and honest. His own interest in politics increased considerably.

> *The things that will destroy America are prosperity-at-any-price, peace-at-any-price, safety first instead of duty first, the love of soft living, and the get-rich-quick theory of life.*
> —THEODORE ROOSEVELT

> *If there is one thing more than another for which I admire you, Theodore, it is your original discovery of the Ten Commandments.*
> —THOMAS B. REED, writer

Theodore had campaigned for Harrison, and although the President disliked the outspoken and brash Roosevelt, he offered him a job. It was low-paying, unglamorous, and sure to win Roosevelt enemies. Yet Theodore gladly accepted his appointment as Civil Service commissioner. It was an ideal position for the dedicated reformer he was becoming.

For years government jobs had been filled by a method known as the "spoils system," in which party membership was the primary job qualification. Whichever party was in power appointed its supporters to available government jobs and dismissed the supporters of the opposition party. The system violated principles of democracy and fair play, but many politicians of both parties did not want to change it. It gave them power and an easy way to reward loyalty.

In 1883 Congress passed the Pendleton Act to abolish the spoils system. But true reform would take more than legislation. It would require strong leadership and dedication on the part of the Civil Service commissioners who had to enforce it. Theodore Roosevelt was clearly the man for the job, and he took to it with his usual enthusiasm.

His job was to see that merit, rather than party membership, was the basis of hiring. To this end, he introduced new and practical tests for job applicants. In addition, he allowed women to compete with men for many positions, a radical idea at the time.

It was a tough challenge, and Roosevelt had to battle many politicians. But the moralistic Theodore always enjoyed fighting for what he thought was right. His dedication was such that when President Harrison was defeated in 1892, the new president, Democrat Grover Cleveland, kept Roosevelt in the job.

However, Theodore Roosevelt's restless mind wanted new challenges. He saw other areas where reforms were needed. In 1894 he was approached to run for mayor of New York on a reform ticket. He declined, saying that he had already run for that job and lost.

The real reason Roosevelt refused the offer was

Theodore Roosevelt with his wife and children in 1903. Roosevelt believed strongly in marriage and the benefits of family life.

the expense of running a political campaign. He was supporting his huge house in Oyster Bay and another household in Washington, D.C., on the remains of his inheritance, a small government salary, and a little income from his writing. He simply didn't have the kind of money a political campaign required. Edith felt especially strongly about this, and Theodore respected her opinions.

Later he deeply regretted his decision not to run

Grover Cleveland, president of the United States from 1893 to 1897. A major issue in the election of 1892 was a surplus in the United States treasury, which Roosevelt, ever the man of action, wanted spent on warships.

for mayor of New York. When Mayor William Strong was elected, Theodore let it be known that he would like a position on the Board of Police Commissioners. In April 1895 Roosevelt and three other new commissioners took office. A month later he was elected president of the board.

Reporters took an immediate liking to the colorful and outspoken Theodore. Wrote one of them: "He has what is essentially a boy's mind. What he thinks he says at once. . . . It is his distinguishing characteristic. However, with it he has great qualities which make him an invaluable public servant— inflexible honesty, absolute fearlessness, and devotion to good government which amounts to religion."

Roosevelt's first concern as board president was corruption in the police department. At that time each job within the department had an unofficial price tag attached to it. To become a captain could cost as much as $10,000; a patrolman's job might cost $300. Whatever the price, however, the money could be quickly recovered by taking bribes from people who wanted to skirt the law. From pushcart peddlers to saloon-keepers, everyone was expected to make a donation to stay on the good side of the police.

Roosevelt fought this brand of corruption. He established a system of appointment and promotion that substituted merit for bribery. He lectured the police on morality and bravery. Many listened, and he gradually built up the morale of the police department.

Roosevelt with the three other members of the New York Board of Police Commissioners in 1895. Roosevelt's drive to wipe out police corruption made him many enemies, but his efforts succeeded.

Roosevelt's experiences as a police commissioner in New York served to change his previous lack of interest in social problems. His exposure to poverty and slum life made him a keen supporter of reform.

Roosevelt also began walking the streets of New York at night to see where the patrolmen were and what they were doing. When he discovered that many were not on the beat, he personally gave them a warning. Second-time offenders were disciplined severely. Within a short time, the streets of New York were indeed safer.

Although Roosevelt was generally a popular figure, he did alienate a large portion of the public with his campaign to enforce a law against drinking in saloons on Sundays. For years the law had been flagrantly ignored. Although Roosevelt had nothing against drinking, he believed that any unenforced law set a bad example and was a source of police corruption. In this case he was right: many saloonkeepers who stayed open on Sunday were guilty of bribery. However, the working class saw Roosevelt's crackdown as an assault on one of their cultural traditions. As a result, his popularity suffered.

Roosevelt became the most controversial figure in New York City. Because of his outspokenness, he often antagonized those who disagreed with him. He always seemed to be in conflict with someone, or everyone. Even the three other commissioners, who had supported him totally at first, began to oppose most of his ideas, and Theodore found himself increasingly thwarted. This was very discouraging for a man of action.

However, nothing could take away his earlier achievements. He had made New York's streets safer, and he had reduced corruption in the police force. When Roosevelt became president of the police commission, a captaincy had cost $10,000; when he left, it cost nothing.

The job had an effect on Roosevelt as well. During his night walks he again encountered the poverty he had first seen in the cigar-makers' tenements. Often he was accompanied by reporters Lincoln Steffens and Jacob Riis, who were writing about the plight of the poor and crusading on their behalf. The two men reinforced his awareness that America was not a land of opportunity for everyone. Roosevelt never forgot these lessons. He was beginning to see that reforming government involved

Crusading journalist Lincoln Steffens greatly influenced Theodore Roosevelt during the 1890s, when his exposure of the plight of America's poor created a public sensation. By 1906 such reporting found less favor with Roosevelt, who suggested that some journalists were "building up a revolutionary feeling."

more than eliminating corruption.

People throughout the country began to recognize Theodore Roosevelt's potential as a leader. Once Jacob Riis asked him if he wanted to be president. The question angered Roosevelt for a moment, but he then admitted thoughtfully, "I must be wanting to be president. Every young man does. But I won't let myself think of it; I must not, because if I do, I will begin to work for it, I'll be careful, calculating, cautious in word and act, and so—I'll beat myself. See?"

He needn't have worried—he was incapable of caution. Bram Stoker, the Englishman who wrote *Dracula*, met Roosevelt around this time and later wrote in his diary, "Must be President some day. A man you can't cajole, can't frighten, can't buy."

In the summer of 1896 Roosevelt toured the country making speeches for Republican presidential candidate William McKinley. When McKinley was elected, Roosevelt let it be known that he would welcome a role in the national government. The conservative McKinley, worried about Roosevelt's reputation for rash words and actions, was reluctant to appoint him to a cabinet position. At the urging of some of Theodore's friends, however, McKinley made him assistant secretary of the navy.

Roosevelt couldn't have been happier. His first book had been a scholarly treatise, *The Naval War of 1812*, and he was convinced that a strong navy was crucial to the United States position as an emerging world power. However, since the end of the Civil War, the fleet had been allowed to deteriorate. Roosevelt worked vigorously in his new position to make the navy stronger. He believed that the United States would soon be at war with Spain over conditions in Cuba, and he wanted the navy to be ready.

Assistant Secretary of the Navy Theodore Roosevelt in 1897. Roosevelt displayed great enthusiasm and initiative in this position. Once, when the secretary of the navy was absent for an afternoon, Roosevelt immediately ordered extensive naval preparations which he thought long overdue.

The *USS Maine* at anchor near Havana, Cuba, shortly before she was blown up on Feb. 15, 1898. The disaster increased anti-Spanish feeling in the United States, with Roosevelt acting as one of the strongest advocates of war with Spain. The inset portrait is of Captain Sigsbee, commander of the *Maine*.

For years the people of Cuba had been in revolt against Spanish rule. Roosevelt felt that it was America's duty to support a democratic revolution there. Although others shared this belief, most political leaders felt that the country should not become involved too deeply in Cuban affairs.

However, the events of February 15, 1898, changed all that. The U.S. battleship *Maine* was anchored just outside the harbor of Havana, Cuba (supposedly there on a courtesy visit). Suddenly an explosion ripped through the ship, killing 262 men. To this day, it is not known who placed the mine that caused the explosion. But Spain was the natural suspect, and sensationalist newspapers in the United States urged war with Spain, coining the slogan "Remember the *Maine*."

While President McKinley tried to negotiate a peaceful settlement, Roosevelt came out strongly on the side of war. Finally, with public opinion demanding revenge, the United States went to war with Spain on April 25, 1898.

Roosevelt was ecstatic. For years he had wanted an opportunity to prove himself in combat. He also wanted his country to show its strength. In a recent speech he had said, "No triumph of peace is quite so great as the supreme triumph of war." When war was declared, he immediately resigned as assistant secretary of the navy and accepted a commission as lieutenant colonel in the First Volunteer Cavalry Regiment, soon to be nicknamed the Rough Riders.

The colonel of the regiment was Roosevelt's good friend Leonard Wood, a young army surgeon. Together they recruited a most unusual assembly of soldiers: cowboys, American Indians, millionaires, miners, Ivy Leaguers, New York City cops—men who had heard about and admired the fighting spirit of Theodore Roosevelt and who shared his ideal of war as the ultimate expression of manliness.

T.R. (as he was often called) was their natural leader and won their respect immediately, though many were shocked at first by his unimpressive size, his glasses, and the formality of his speech. His leadership also proved unconventional. Typical Roosevelt high spirits didn't always jibe with regular army discipline. On one occasion Colonel Wood soundly reprimanded him for treating an entire squadron to unlimited amounts of beer in a San Antonio saloon as a reward for their improvement in drill.

After training, the Rough Riders sailed for Cuba. On July 1, 1898, came Roosevelt's supreme moment of glory, the charge up Kettle Hill in the battle of San Juan Hill. He himself called it his

Colonel Leonard Wood, commanding officer of the First Volunteer Cavalry, under whom Roosevelt served in Cuba in 1898. Roosevelt's larger-than-life personality tended to obscure Wood's higher rank, and the regiment became known to soldiers and civilians alike simply as Roosevelt's Rough Riders.

"crowded hour," and it did prove that Theodore Roosevelt was a courageous and inspired leader of men.

At the same time, the battle revealed the serious flaws to which Roosevelt's passions could lead him. He spoke with pride of the casualties his men had sustained, and he positively gloated over the dead Spanish soldiers. For the rest of his life he never tired of telling the story in terms that could only be called boastful. One writer commented that Roosevelt's writings about the war should have been called "Alone in Cuba."

As the war in Cuba quickly neared an end, Roosevelt became aware that the greatest enemy of his men was disease. With the support of other officers, he wrote to McKinley and his secretary of the army, urging them to recall the troops since the Spanish

American troops parading prior to embarking for Cuba during the Spanish-American War. Neither side particularly distinguished itself in Cuba. The Spaniards suffered poor leadership, while the combination of regular and volunteer regiments in the American forces created inconsistencies in the conduct of the campaign. Volunteer units expected the full support of regular troops in actions which the regulars thought reckless.

Cuban soldiers who were loyal to Spain prepare for action during the Spanish-American War. Cuban insurgency against the Spanish government began in 1895, ruining America's trade with Cuba ($100 million in 1894). This consideration, allied with América's opposition to European influence in the Caribbean, made war inevitable.

were clearly defeated. When the President did not act immediately, Roosevelt took his opinions to the newspapers. McKinley was furious. As a result, Theodore never received the Medal of Honor he deserved and desperately wanted.

Roosevelt returned to Long Island with his Rough Riders in August 1898. He was the hero of the Spanish-American War and the most famous man in America. Much of the acclaim was deserved, but some of it was the result of his almost constant self-promotion. He was enthusiastic about every-

You had to hate the Colonel a whole lot to keep from loving him.
—IRVIN S. COBB, writer

ROUGH RIDERS. COL. THEODORE ROOSEVELT, U.S.V. COMMANDER.

An artist's conception of Theodore Roosevelt and the Rough Riders in action during the Spanish-American War. Their first engagement in Cuba occurred when Spanish and American cavalry units met unintentionally. Roosevelt's regiment suffered 66 casualties, but he insisted that "we wanted the first whack at the Spaniards and we got it."

The instant I received the order I sprang on my horse, and then my "crowded hour" began [the battle of Kettle Hill].
—THEODORE ROOSEVELT

Only those are fit to live who do not fear to die; and none are fit to die who have shrunk from the joy of life and the duty of life. Both life and death are part of the same Great Adventure.
—THEODORE ROOSEVELT

thing, including his own achievements.

With the war over and glory achieved, Roosevelt wanted to get back into politics. It had been more than ten years since he had run for an elective office. The Republican Party in New York, facing certain defeat, was looking for a popular hero to save the governorship. T.R. was clearly the man. The only obstacle was "Boss" Thomas C. Platt, the undisputed leader of New York Republicans. (A political boss is someone who controls a local party organization.)

Like all political bosses of the time, Platt wanted a governor he could control easily. He was smart enough to realize that Theodore Roosevelt did not fill the bill. But he also recognized the war hero's vote-getting appeal. In the end, Platt decided that having a Republican governor outweighed the difficulty of controlling Roosevelt after the election.

Roosevelt campaigned vigorously, often with fellow Rough Riders at his side to liven up rallies and speeches. The voters loved it and Roosevelt won easily. After the election he and Boss Platt managed an uneasy truce.

Theodore Roosevelt was beginning to learn an essential fact of politics—the art of compromise. It had been the one ingredient lacking in his recipe for political success. It took the kind of humility that T.R. did not possess in large quantities, but he was beginning to see its importance. By compromising with Boss Platt, he was able to appoint honest men to important positions in New York State.

In spite of Roosevelt's compromises, Boss Platt was not happy with a maverick reformer in the governor's seat. As a result, when the presidential election of 1900 neared, Platt began a movement to have Roosevelt nominated for vice-president under McKinley, who was running for a second term.

Roosevelt himself leaned strongly toward another term as governor instead of the thankless and largely ceremonial job of vice-president. At one point he wrote, "Most emphatically the vice-presidential nomination is the last thing I want. I would rather be professor of history in some college." But friends

United States army engineers on maneuvers in Cuba following the Spanish-American War.

Theodore Roosevelt and President McKinley discuss their plans for the election campaign of 1900. Republicans in the western United States had helped secure Roosevelt's vice-presidential nomination to offset McKinley's extreme political conservatism.

pointed out that he would be in an excellent position to run for president in 1904 if he accepted the vice-presidency. It was difficult for a man of action to give up present power for the possibility of greater power in the future. Roosevelt finally gave in to a swell of popular support and consented to be McKinley's running mate.

While President McKinley campaigned from the front porch of his home in Ohio, Roosevelt crisscrossed the country, denouncing William Jennings Bryan, the Democratic candidate. The Republicans won, and in March 1901 Roosevelt was sworn in as vice-president, resigned to four years of boredom and inaction.

In September while attending an outing of the Vermont Fish and Game League, Roosevelt received the startling news that President McKinley had been shot at the Pan-American Exposition in Buffalo, New York. Roosevelt hurried to the scene. After five days doctors decided that McKinley was out of danger. To reassure the country that there was no need for alarm, the vice-president joined his family on vacation in the Adirondack Mountains.

On September 13 the Roosevelts were eating lunch atop a mountain when a messenger arrived with

Roosevelt speaks during the presidential election campaign of 1900, when he was McKinley's running mate on the Republican ticket. Demonstrating his usual tirelessness, Roosevelt made 673 speeches and traveled 20,000 miles during the campaign.

> *I have a definite philosophy about the presidency. I think it should be a very powerful office, and I think the president should be a very strong man who uses without hesitation every power that the position yields.*
>
> —THEODORE ROOSEVELT

William Jennings Bryan, the Democratic presidential candidate in 1900. Roosevelt hated Bryan's politics, which favored aiding minorities, as well as his proposed economic policies, which, said Roosevelt, "would paralyze our whole industrial life."

the news that McKinley was dying. Roosevelt raced for the bottom of the mountain. A rickety horse-drawn buckboard was hunted up, and T.R. spent a bumpy night en route to Buffalo. When he arrived McKinley was dead.

On September 14, 1901, at the age of 42, Theodore Roosevelt became the youngest president in the history of the United States.

Roosevelt confers with a local Republican in Buffalo, New York, shortly after the assassination of President McKinley. During the nine days between the shooting and McKinley's death, Roosevelt was little concerned with the prospect of becoming president.

3

That Cowboy in the White House

Theodore Roosevelt had been enjoying himself all his life, and he wasn't about to stop just because he was now President. Certain things had always been important to him. He made sure there was room for them in his new routine. Physical activity, family, friends, books, nature—these were some of the pleasures that made living worthwhile.

As President, T.R. set aside two hours a day for exercise. Occasionally he fenced with his old Rough Rider friend Leonard Wood. Sometimes he took boxing lessons, until in 1904 an injury caused him to lose sight in his left eye. After that he took up Japanese wrestling.

Often the President led cabinet members, congressmen, and diplomats on rambles through Rock Creek Park in Washington. These were no sedate sightseeing tours, though. They were "point-to-point" walks: to get from the starting point to the finishing point, you could go over, under, but not around any object that got in your way.

With the President in the lead, a group of grown men would scramble up hills, climb over rocks, and sometimes even swim across streams until they returned to the White House huffing and

John D. Rockefeller, in 1890. When Rockefeller's Standard Oil Trust was dissolved in 1899, Roosevelt disclosed that a Rockefeller aide had asked United States senators to vote against the creation of new antitrust legislation.

Theodore Roosevelt campaigns in 1900, as McKinley's running mate on the Republican ticket. The enthusiasm shown for Roosevelt convinced many that he might one day become president himself.

puffing, often with their clothes in a sorry state. The President's characteristic evaluation: "Wasn't that bully!" "Bully" was his all-purpose word of approval.

It wasn't just with friends and politicians that Roosevelt enjoyed himself. At heart he remained a boy and always enjoyed the company of children. He often appeared in the White House nursery for the before-dinner story hour when Edith read to

Theodore Roosevelt enjoys the strenuous life during a riding holiday.

the younger children. He would listen with rapt attention to the wife he adored. When the stories were finished, he might start a vigorous pillow fight. After a good romp the President often had to change his shirt to be presentable for a formal state dinner.

The Roosevelt children made the White House the most lively one since Abraham Lincoln's two boys had been there in the 1860s. Alice, the oldest, was 17, and a high-spirited, outspoken beauty. The press called her Princess Alice, and the public couldn't get enough news about her outrageous doings.

The President himself loved her wit, courage, and intolerance of anything dull. She was a "chip off the old block," though she could be trying. Once when Alice had dashed in and out of the President's office three times in a short period, a visitor asked, "Isn't there anything you can do to control Alice?" T.R. replied, "I can do one of two things. I can be President of the United States, or I can control Alice. I can't possibly do both."

Ted and Kermit, 12 and 14 when their father became President, were away at boarding school, but Ethel, Archie, and Quentin quickly made themselves at home in the White House. They roller-skated in the basement, walked on stilts through the high-ceilinged rooms, and kept the wide assortment of pets that were always part of a Roosevelt household.

Eventually the White House staff got used to the unpredictable nature of life with the Roosevelts. So there was not much fuss when Quentin decided to cheer up 9-year-old Archie, who was recovering from measles and whooping cough, by bringing him a 350-pound pony. With the help of a footman, the nervous pony was coaxed into an elevator and was soon trotting into the invalid's second-floor bedroom.

T.R.'s enjoyment of family, friends, and the strenuous life did not mean that he ignored the responsibilities of being president. In fact, hard work was one of the ways that Theodore Roosevelt enjoyed himself. At the turn of the century, the United States and the world were changing dramatically.

... he was so alive at all points, and so gifted with the rare faculty of living intensely and entirely in every moment as it passed. ...
—EDITH WHARTON

No president had ever enjoyed himself as much as I.
—THEODORE ROOSEVELT

PRESIDENT ASTONISHES FINANCIERS

Mr. Roosevelt Directs Attorney General Knox to Bring Suit to Dissolve the Northern Securities Merger.

BILL IN EQUITY SOON TO BE FILED

J. Pierpont Morgan, James J. Hill and Their Associates Will Be Made the Defendants.

Morgan   Hill   Harriman

NEW YORK MARCH 15, 1904.

SUPREME COURT WRECKS MERGER

Northern Securities Company an Unlawful Combination.

Following a Roosevelt trust-busting initiative in 1902, a 1904 Supreme Court decision declared the Northern Securities company in violation of anti-trust law. The debate about the role of government in relation to business continues to this day.

A president who wanted to work hard could find plenty of work to do.

Since the end of the Civil War, America had experienced tremendous economic growth. A country that had been primarily agricultural was quickly becoming the most advanced industrial nation in the world. Oil, steel, coal, manufacturing, and railroads were all big business.

Entrepreneurs like John D. Rockefeller, J. Pierpont Morgan, and Andrew Carnegie were amassing enormous fortunes through bold business ventures. They believed that what was good for big business was good for America. And Congress, conservative and strongly influenced by the power of money, believed it too. As a result, there was little government regulation of business.

Theodore Roosevelt had nothing against business or making money. His own ancestors had done quite well. But the financial success of the Roosevelts had been based on integrity and service. In addition, Roosevelt's father had taught him that the rich had a moral obligation to help the less fortunate. So Roosevelt developed a strong contempt for those he called the "criminal rich," greedy businessmen who recognized no principle other than their own right to make as much money as possible.

One business practice the President considered immoral was the formation of trusts. A trust was a combination of companies formed especially for the purpose of reducing competition. For example, if several large oil companies formed a trust, they could set a fixed price for their product. This would eliminate the possibility that one company in the trust would undersell another. Without price competition, of course, consumers would have to pay whatever price the trust established.

As President, Roosevelt could not pass laws against unfair business practices, but he could enforce the few laws that already existed. In 1890 Congress, seeing that trusts could operate against the public welfare, had passed the Sherman Antitrust Act. But the law had not been widely enforced. Roosevelt, as President, now saw an opportunity to put his beliefs into action. In short order he went after the trusts.

Archie (saluting) and Quentin Roosevelt line up with the White House police. President Roosevelt's children inherited their father's exuberance and greatly contributed to the informality of the Roosevelt White House.

Andrew Carnegie, millionaire and philanthropist, a leading figure in American business during the 1890s and early 1900s.

Five weeks after Roosevelt took office, the railroad owners James J. Hill, J.P. Morgan, and Edward H. Harriman joined forces to form the Northern Securities Company, a railroad trust that eliminated competition in the Northwest. The result was that shippers had to pay extremely high prices to get their goods to market. Roosevelt decided that Northern Securities was clearly violating the Sherman Antitrust Act, and he asked the courts to prosecute the trust.

The business community reacted with astonishment and dismay. As one newspaper put it, "Wall Street is paralyzed at the thought that a President of the United States would sink so low as to try to enforce the law." Morgan himself paid a call at the White House to impress the President with the gravity of the situation. But the President did not budge.

The trust was not about to give in easily, however, and the court battles went on for years. Finally, in 1904, the Supreme Court ruled against the Northern Securities Company, and Theodore Roosevelt was on his way to earning the nickname "Trust-Buster." During his presidency 25 trusts were indicted under the Sherman Antitrust Act, and never again did big business have unchecked power to do what it wanted.

President Roosevelt did not want to destroy

Theodore Roosevelt with workers in 1917. In the early 1900s some Roosevelt opponents considered his interest in worker welfare almost socialistic.

President Roosevelt prepares to hand out diplomas at the United States Naval Academy in Annapolis in 1902. His interest in naval affairs continued throughout his life.

business. He viewed it as the country's new frontier and a potential force for good. There were exciting new ideas and tremendous energy in business. And Roosevelt was not a man to downplay ideas and energy. But he wanted to make sure that a majority of the people benefited from the new industrial giants. He believed one way to accomplish this was to have government regulate business. It was a radical idea at the time, but he did convince Congress to include a Bureau of Corporations in the newly formed Department of Commerce and Labor.

Labor was another new force at the turn of the

century. Immigrants arriving daily by the boatloads
provided cheap labor for new businesses. Poor and
eager for work, many immigrants accepted without
question the policies of their employers. But many
employers were more interested in making money
than providing safe working conditions or fair
salaries.

Eventually labor unions formed to claim the right
to negotiate with management for better pay and
working conditions. For its part, big business fought
with all its strength and resources to break the
unions.

One of Roosevelt's first crises after taking office

**Immigration from Europe
to the United States be-
came a major political
issue in the early 20th
century. Although many
immigrants accepted low-
paid work in bad condi-
tions they eventually
formed unions and de-
manded a voice in politics.**

was a strike by anthracite coal miners in Pennsylvania. The union was seeking an increase in wages, improved conditions in the mines, and recognition as a bargaining agent. The attitude of the owners was exemplified in a comment by industrialist George Baer, who claimed that the miners "don't suffer; why, they can't even speak English."

Roosevelt believed that the anthracite coal industry was a trust. He also knew that the strike was causing great hardship for vast numbers of people who needed coal to heat homes, schools, hospitals, and offices. After repeated efforts to bring the two sides together failed, the President threatened to send federal troops to operate the mines.

In 1902 such government intervention in business matters was unheard of. When one of Roosevelt's advisors cautioned that this action might be unconstitutional, T.R. grabbed him by the shoulder and exclaimed, "The Constitution was made for the people and not the people for the Constitution."

The strike was finally settled by arbitration, without the intervention of federal troops. However, in threatening to use the power of the federal government against big business and on behalf of the public, Roosevelt took a bold step in a new direction.

In foreign affairs, his actions were also characterized by a bold approach. He felt it was time for the United States to adopt a strong stance as a world leader. In part his philosophy came from his own lifelong impulse for power and control. And in part it stemmed from his conviction that he and the United States were inevitably on the side of right. Furthermore he felt that the more "advanced" countries had an obligation to lead the more "backward." This attitude, while now considered self-righteous and condescending, was not unusual for that time.

His foreign policy came to be expressed in the slogan "Speak softly and carry a big stick." To Roosevelt that meant always being willing to negotiate and hold back from rash actions, yet always having the power to back words with deeds. This policy was most often tested in relations with European countries over events in Latin America.

Theodore Roosevelt speaks to suffragettes in New York in 1917. His views on women's rights changed constantly. As early as 1880 he wrote, "...it is advisable to make women equal to men before the law."

President Roosevelt was determined to demonstrate American military might to the whole world. Here, in 1907, elements of the United States Navy's battle fleet assemble prior to conducting a global voyage.

The United States had always had a special interest in her southern neighbors. In 1823 President James Monroe had proclaimed the Monroe Doctrine, which warned that the United States would not allow European nations to colonize or interfere in Latin America.

At the turn of the century many European countries were concerned about debts owed them by Latin American nations. They considered it their right to collect on these debts, by force if necessary. At first Roosevelt agreed, but soon it became apparent that a European nation trying to force repayment might easily use the opportunity to seize territory. That would be a violation of the Monroe Doctrine.

In 1904 Roosevelt proclaimed what became known as the Roosevelt Corollary to the Monroe Doctrine. (A corollary is something that logically follows from something else.) The Roosevelt Corollary asserted that if a Latin American country could not manage its financial affairs so as to avoid invasion by other powers, it was the right and duty of the United States to intervene.

The Roosevelt Corollary was put to the test in 1905 when President Morales of the Dominican Republic agreed to allow the United States to take over the collection of customs (import and export taxes that were supposed to be used to pay off the country's foreign debts). European countries were clamoring for repayment, and Morales wanted to avoid invasion. Roosevelt appointed a collector of customs from the United States, and financial stability was restored to the Dominican Republic.

Many people opposed the Roosevelt Corollary, believing that the United States should stay out of the affairs of other nations. And in the long run Roosevelt's policy of intervention did cause deep resentments in Latin America.

Strangely, the man who gloried in war and believed that developed countries should lead less

President Roosevelt reviews American troops in the Panama Canal zone in November 1906.

developed nations did not want the United States to build an empire, as many European powers were doing at the time. Roosevelt opposed the taking of colonies for economic benefit.

Thus, in 1902 he withdrew American troops from Cuba, granting that country the independence he had fought to attain. As a result of the war with Spain, the United States had also acquired the Philippines, but Roosevelt consistently maintained that America's role there was to prepare the people for self-government.

However, as always, Roosevelt operated on the principle that he knew best; and in his opinion the Philippines were not yet ready for independence. So, when United States troops brutally put down a Philippine independence movement, the President supported the action.

Perhaps T.R.'s greatest achievement in foreign policy was to begin the Panama Canal. For hundreds of years people had dreamed of building a canal across the narrowest part of Central America. Such a canal would link the Atlantic and Pacific oceans, so that ships would no longer have to go around South America.

Roosevelt also saw the military advantages in such a canal. The United States Navy would be in a stronger position if ships could get from one ocean to the other quickly. In his view a canal would thus contribute to the emergence of the United States as a world power.

In 1903 the United States began to negotiate with Colombia for rights to build a canal across the Isthmus of Panama, which was then a province of Colombia. Complex negotiations were broken off when Roosevelt claimed that Colombia was backing down from terms already agreed upon.

Eventually Washington received word that Pana-

President Roosevelt takes a seat inside a huge steam-powered shovel in Panama in 1906, during the construction of the Panama Canal. Roosevelt once said he had intended to occupy Panama anyway, regardless of the Panamanian revolution against Colombia which he used as an excuse for intervention in 1903.

Sagamore Hill, the Roosevelt family home on Long Island, New York.

manian revolutionaries were on the verge of declaring independence from Colombia. On November 4, 1903, United States Marines landed at Colon in Panama and prevented Colombian troops from going to Panama City to put down the rebellion.

The revolution was quickly over, and Panamanians who favored the United States came to power. Shortly afterwards Panama signed an agreement permitting the United States to build the canal. Although technically the United States did not take part in the revolution, T.R. later said, "I took the isthmus." No one seems to have disputed his claim.

Acquiring land rights was just the beginning of problems in building the Panama Canal. When construction bogged down because of disease and disorganization and Congress refused to act, Roosevelt reorganized the project by executive order. He gave the construction job to the United States Army and appointed a director who saw the job to completion in 1914.

In his three years as President, Theodore Roose-

At Sagamore Hill we love a great many things—birds and trees and books, and all things beautiful, and horses and rifles and children and hard work and the joy of life.
—THEODORE ROOSEVELT

President Theodore Roosevelt was inaugurated on March 4, 1905. Although many prominent businessmen had financed his election campaign, Roosevelt displayed characteristic independence, emphasizing the importance of regulating big business.

velt had put his very personal mark on the domestic and foreign policies of the United States. He was propelling the country into the 20th century by the force of his own strong will.

Many disagreed with his policies, especially the conservative members of Congress. To them he was an unpredictable wild man. When T.R. took office, McKinley's good friend Senator Mark Hanna had remarked, "Now look, that damned cowboy is President of the United States." And there were many who scoffed with him. Roosevelt's aggressive use of power had made him enemies, especially in big business. In 1904 he seriously wondered if he could be elected President in his own right.

He need not have worried. The people loved him. They could not get enough of him and the lively first family. Reporters trailed "Princess" Alice as she took a ride in a submarine or traveled by car from Newport to Boston at the reckless speed of 25 miles an hour or smoked cigarettes in public.

While Alice was a delicious scandal, Edith Roosevelt was the perfect First Lady and hostess. She had overseen renovations and redecoration that restored the White House to a more classical style. There and at Sagamore Hill, the "summer White House," she graciously presided over exciting parties.

During previous administrations it was mainly businessmen and politicians who had visited the executive mansion. Now artists, writers, scientists, people with new and exciting ideas were invited to dine with the First Family. All in all there was an excitement about the Roosevelt White House, and the people were enchanted.

In spite of his popular support, T.R. campaigned vigorously and with his usual enthusiasm. For one thing, he believed in leaving nothing to chance. And he genuinely enjoyed contact with the American people.

Roosevelt defeated his Democratic opponent, Alton Parker, by an overwhelming margin. Now he truly believed that the people supported his ideas. But he would have difficulty putting them into practice, as Congress was still ruled by conservatives.

Also, some people believed that Roosevelt had

made a serious mistake by announcing that he would not run for a third term in 1908. As a result, his opponents in Congress knew four years in advance that he would not be taking his cause to the people again. So every piece of legislation he wanted had to be carefully negotiated with congressional conservatives. And there was still plenty the President wanted.

On the home front, he went ahead with programs that he had begun to call the "Square Deal." His objective was a more just society in which special privileges would be struck down and big business regulated.

As part of the Square Deal, he pushed through Congress the Hepburn Act of 1906. This gave the Interstate Commerce Commission the authority to set maximum rates for railroads. He also pressed

Gifford Pinchot at a ceremony initiating the construction of a dam in Pennsylvania. Pinchot, an ardent conservationist, was appointed head of the United States Forest Service by Theodore Roosevelt, a position from which he was dismissed in 1910 by President Taft.

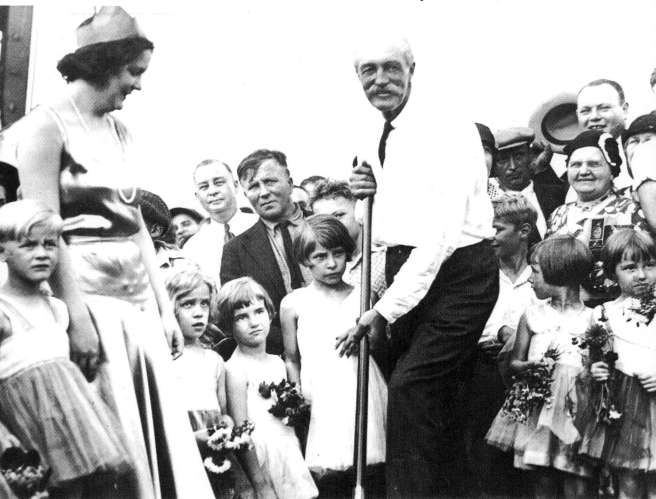

Theodore Roosevelt relaxes during a hunting trip in Colorado in 1905. Always concerned with maintaining his image as an expert hunter, Roosevelt insisted that on his trip he should make the first kill.

Congress for a Pure Food and Drug Act and for legislation regulating the meat-packing industry.

Roosevelt's awareness of unsanitary practices in meat-packing plants had come from *The Jungle,* a book by Upton Sinclair. Sinclair belonged to a group of crusading journalists who attempted to expose corruption and injustice in America. T.R. called them "muckrakers," one of several words he added to the language. He disliked their negative outlook but learned a great deal from them.

Perhaps Roosevelt's most lasting achievement as President was to preserve for posterity a large portion of America's land. As far back as his days in the Badlands, he had seen the need for conservation. When he became President, he appointed ardent conservationist Gifford Pinchot to head the United States Forest Service.

During his administrations Roosevelt added 230 million acres to the lands owned by the United States government and protected from unregulated development. He doubled the number of national parks, created the first 50 national wildlife refuges and the first 18 national monuments.

Roosevelt's conservation efforts were among his most controversial policies. Congress, upset that the President was using executive power to achieve his conservation goals, passed a bill saying that only Congress could create or expand forest reserves in six Western states. In the few weeks before the bill took effect, Roosevelt and Pinchot gleefully worked round the clock to create new reserves with a total of 16 million acres.

Some have found it difficult to reconcile the President's conservation measures with his love of hunting. But as naturalist John Burroughs once said, "Such a hunter as Roosevelt is as far removed from the game-butcher as day is from night." One of the classic T.R. stories confirms Burroughs' opinion.

Once, on a bear-hunting trip in Mississippi, the President was having no luck. Some members of his party caught an old blind bear and tied it to a tree for Roosevelt to shoot. The President was disgusted and insisted that the bear be let loose. When reporters heard the story, they filled the newspapers with it. Political cartoonist Clifford Berryman drew a cartoon that showed Roosevelt refusing to shoot a bear cub. The cub became a T.R. trademark, and within a short time toy manufacturers had come out with the "Teddy bear" (though Roosevelt himself hated the nickname Teddy).

Another area in which Roosevelt broke new ground was civil rights. His sincere admiration for individual achievement prevented him from discriminating against any person. He was the first President to appoint a Jew, Secretary of Labor and Commerce Oscar Straus, to his cabinet. He also sought ways to bring blacks into the Republican Party in the South. At his invitation Booker T. Washington became the first black to dine at the White House.

However, human rights was not a burning issue at the turn of the century, and even Roosevelt was not immune to the racial and ethnic stereotyping then prevalent.

Booker T. Washington in 1894. A leading educator, Washington worked hard during the 1890s to build a new Republican organization in which advancement was gained by achievement, not bribery. Such ideals soon brought him to Roosevelt's attention.

President Theodore Roosevelt with gunners on board the *USS Texas* in 1903.

Though he believed that immigrants should be treated fairly, he also felt that immigration to the United States should be limited. And he was strongly criticized for severely punishing some black soldiers who had been accused of criminal acts but had not been tried or convicted. Roosevelt defended his actions as necessary to uphold the standards of the army, but the whole affair left a bad impression on many fair-minded people.

In his second term Roosevelt turned his foreign policy efforts toward the Far East. He had two goals, both intended to continue the "Open Door" policy first announced under President McKinley. One was to make sure that no one nation dominated the Far East. The second was to see that no nation interfered with profitable United States trade relations with China. To achieve these goals, he looked to Japan to provide a balance of power. By supporting Japan he hoped to keep Russia and other European nations from gaining too much influence in the Far East.

In 1904 Russia and Japan went to war. Roosevelt initiated peace talks at an opportune moment for Japan. Meeting with representatives of the two countries on the presidential yacht off Oyster Bay, he laid the groundwork for harmonious negotiations. Ultimately the Treaty of Portsmouth established peace. In 1906 Roosevelt became the first American to receive the Nobel Peace Prize. His prestige at home and abroad soared.

T.R. could be a peacemaker at times, but his foreign policy was still summed up in the phrase "Speak softly and carry a big stick." To show off the big stick, in 1907 he sent the United States Navy on a cruise. The ships were all painted white, and the prominence of the Great White Fleet did

An artist's impression of a naval engagement during the war between Russia and Japan in 1904–5. Roosevelt's mediation of the dispute ended the conflict on terms satisfactory to both sides. Historian Henry Adams congratulated Roosevelt, calling him "the best herder of emperors since Napoleon."

Japanese troops burn their dead during the Russo-Japanese War. Roosevelt believed that America's interests in the Far East were best served by a balance of power between Russia and Japan.

Roosevelt negotiates the end of the Russo-Japanese War in 1905. With him (left to right) are Count Witte and Baron Rosen of Russia, and Baron Komura and Minister Takahira of Japan.

much to establish the United States as a power in the eyes of the world.

Roosevelt kept his pledge not to run for reelection in 1908. Instead he gave his support to his secretary of war, William Howard Taft, who easily beat the Democratic candidate, William Jennings Bryan.

Aboard the *USS Connecticut*, President Roosevelt speaks at the conclusion of the famous "Great White Fleet" cruise of 1907–9. Germany's Admiral von Tirpitz told Roosevelt in 1910 that he had quite expected the Japanese navy to attack the American fleet. Instead, Japan exercised diplomacy and welcomed the American ships.

While the inauguration festivities were still going on, Theodore and Edith Roosevelt quietly slipped out of Washington. They were bound for Sagamore Hill and the private life that Edith cherished. A snowstorm delayed them, but when they arrived at the train station at 1:00 A.M., an enthusiastic band of young people was waiting to welcome them home.

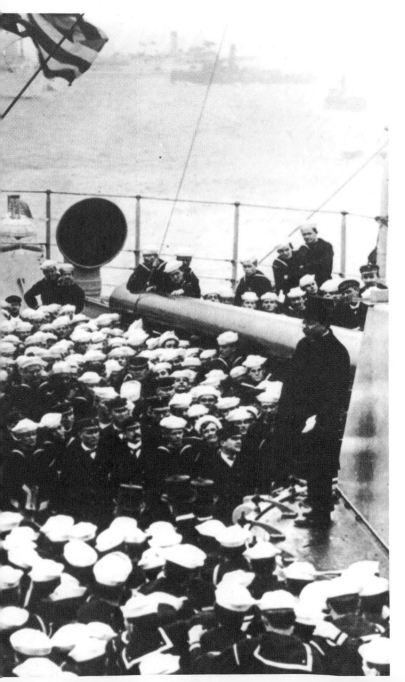

Much has been given us, and much will rightfully be expected from us . . . We have become a great nation, forced by the fact of its greatness into relations with the other nations of the earth, and we must behave as beseems a people with such responsibilities.
—THEODORE ROOSEVELT

4

The Bull Moose

The cowboy in the White House was once again a private citizen. At the age of 50, however, Theodore Roosevelt was not about to give up the strenuous life and disappear into quiet retirement. Friends made suggestions. Some thought he would make an ideal university president. Others believed he should run for Congress, as John Quincy Adams had done after his presidency. One cabinet member, noting Roosevelt's tendency to preach, jokingly suggested that he should be made a bishop.

T.R. himself was sure of one thing: "When I stop being President I will stop completely." He added that he was "under no temptation to snatch at the fringes of departing glory." It was a resolution more easily made than kept. For if Theodore Roosevelt did not "snatch" at glory, glory—or at least public attention—often turned around and snatched at him.

Perhaps to remove himself from temptation, even before he left office he began to plan an expedition into the heart of Africa. The trip would have two benefits. It would be a great adventure for the dedicated naturalist, and it would make him completely unavailable for comment on political events. This would enable Taft to start his presidency without the newspapers constantly seeking Roosevelt's views.

President Roosevelt in the White House in 1908.

William Howard Taft, 27th president of the United States, was secretary of war during the second Roosevelt administration, and became the Republican presidential candidate in 1908 at Roosevelt's personal recommendation.

Theodore Roosevelt with one of the victims of his 1909 hunting and scientific expedition to Africa.

Roosevelt set sail for Africa on March 23, 1909, a little over two weeks after leaving office. He had planned a scientific expedition as well as a hunting trip, so he brought along three field naturalists and taxidermists from the Smithsonian Institution. Also in the party was Roosevelt's second son, Kermit, who took off a year from Harvard to accompany the group as photographer. T.R.'s rule was that they would shoot only what was needed for museum specimens or for food.

As usual on a Roosevelt "vacation," T.R. was rarely at rest. By night he sat near the campfire at a portable desk, writing the day's events in his diary. These accounts were eventually published as articles by *Scribner's* magazine and later as a book, *African Game Trails.* When not writing, Roosevelt had his nose in a book. He took along a library of

60 volumes, ranging from Shakespeare's plays to *Alice's Adventures in Wonderland.*

But it was during the days of tracking and shooting that the former president was happiest. He himself admitted that he was not a great shot. His vision, never good, was now limited to his right eye. He often needed several shots to kill his prey, but he seldom let a wounded animal escape.

T.R.'s goal was to bag the five most dangerous game animals: elephant, rhinoceros, buffalo, leopard, and lion. He did much more than that. By trip's end he had shot 9 lions, 8 elephants, 13 rhinoceroses, 6 buffaloes, and 53 other species—a total of 296 animals. Kermit bagged a total of 216 animals, including the rare leopard. The two Roosevelts kept about a dozen trophies for themselves. The rest went to the Smithsonian.

On the trip, Roosevelt also observed small mammals called tree hyraxes. To his amusement he was informed that these "squat, woolly, funny things" were known among the local white settlers as "Teddy bears." It seemed that his popularity knew no boundaries.

The safari ended in February 1910 when the party met Edith and Ethel Roosevelt in Khartoum. The family then embarked on a grand tour of Egypt and Europe, where they were royally entertained. In Oslo, Norway, Roosevelt accepted the Nobel Prize he had been awarded in 1906 for his role in settling the Russo-Japanese War. By previous invitation, he delivered lectures at leading universities (the Sorbonne in Paris and Oxford in England). Then, chancing to be in England when King Edward VII died, he represented President Taft at the funeral.

In June 1910 the former president returned to an enthusiastic reception in New York. Though he had vowed he would not "snatch at departing glory," he could not avoid attention. A parade in his honor included former Rough Riders, mounted police, and a police band. An estimated one million people lined the streets. One bystander kept shouting into a megaphone, "Our next President."

During his safari Roosevelt had been cut off from

Theodore Roosevelt cultivates his image as an explorer. When he returned from Africa in 1910, publishers stampeded for the rights to his account of his travels, a situation which caused England's King Edward VII to refer to the hapless Roosevelt as a "penny a line writer."

Theodore Roosevelt with Gifford Pinchot (at left) in 1910. President Taft's dismissal of Pinchot from the Forest Service that year upset Roosevelt, although he later admitted that Pinchot's blunders during congressional investigations of the Department of the Interior had made the dismissal necessary.

I believe that the natural resources must be used for the benefit of all of our people and not monopolized for the benefit of the few.
—THEODORE ROOSEVELT

"I'VE GOT TO SEE HIM!"

A political cartoon from the Roosevelt era makes the point that throughout his political career the Republicans considered Roosevelt essential both to their unity and their capacity to attract votes.

the news. As he began catching up with events of the day he became increasingly displeased with Taft's policies. In general, Taft was more conservative, more willing to go along with the Republican Party's Old Guard and with big business. In particular, Taft had undermined or ignored Roosevelt's conservation policies. He had added insult to injury by firing T.R.'s friend Gifford Pinchot as head of the Forest Service.

Roosevelt also found the Republican Party sharply divided between the conservative Old Guard and a new breed of reformers who called themselves Progressives. Progressives held the optimistic belief that the United States could become a land of greater opportunity for all. They favored government regulation of big business and programs that would help laborers and small businesses.

As senior statesman of his party, Roosevelt considered it his duty to unite the conservatives and Progressives. To do so, he toured the country making speeches in support of all Republican candidates for Congress. But one of these speeches made clear his growing support for the Progressive movement.

On August 31, 1910, dedicating the John Brown Battlefield at Osawatomie, Kansas, Roosevelt argued forcefully for a stronger national government that would put human rights before property rights. Others had called this philosophy the New Nationalism. In supporting it, T.R. took his Square Deal a step further.

He maintained, "When I say that I am for the square deal I mean not merely that I stand for fair play under the present rules of the game, but that I stand for having those rules changed so as to work for a more substantial equality of opportunity and of reward for equally good service."

The Osawatomie speech pointed up the widening gap between Roosevelt and Taft. As the election of 1912 neared, Republican Progressives began to turn to Roosevelt to carry their banner. His name was put in nomination at the Republican convention. It was clear that many people were still behind the hero of the Spanish-American War. But the Old

Guard controlled the convention, and Taft was nominated as the Republican candidate.

The 344 delegates pledged to Roosevelt angrily stormed out of the convention, formed the American Progressive Party, and made Roosevelt their presidential candidate. When asked about his physical fitness for the campaign ahead, Roosevelt replied that he felt as "strong as a bull moose." He thus gave the new party its unofficial name, the Bull Moose Party.

Roosevelt soon proved just how sound of body he was. Near the end of the campaign, as he was leaving a Milwaukee hotel to make a speech, he was suddenly shot in the chest by a former New York City saloon-keeper named John Chrank, who was later judged to be insane. Refusing to cancel the speech, the candidate addressed the crowd for an hour and a half. Only then did he agree to be treated for the wound. The bullet broke a rib and narrowly missed his heart. Fortunately, its impact was lessened by an eyeglass case in his vest pocket,

Roosevelt and companions during the Brazilian expedition of 1913. The expedition was a scientific and geographical success, and also worked well for public relations. Crowds welcomed Roosevelt throughout his trip, suggesting that many South Americans did not resent the American's presence in Panama.

but doctors agreed that his excellent physical condition probably saved his life.

True to his nature, Roosevelt made the Bull Moose campaign a moral crusade. In his nomination speech he declared, "Our cause is based on the eternal principles of righteousness. We stand at Armageddon, and we battle for the Lord."

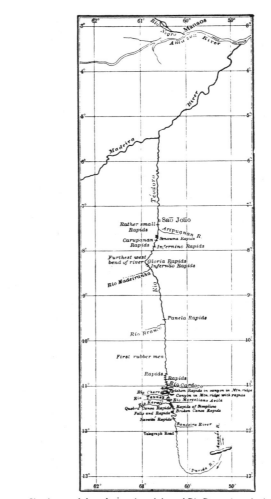

Sketch map of the unknown river christened Rio Roosevelt, and subsequently Rio Téodoro, by direction of the Brazilian Government

This map was prepared by Colonel Roosevelt from his journal and the diaries of Cherrie and of Kermit Roosevelt, the war having prevented the arrival of the map prepared by Lieutenant Lyra The Ananás may be the headwaters of the Cardozo or of the Aripuanan, or it may flow into the Canuma or Tapajos; it will not be put on the map until it is actually descended

An extract from Roosevelt's book *Through the Brazilian Wilderness*. The map shows the previously uncharted river which he explored and which was later named after him by the Brazil's government.

Woodrow Wilson, President of the United States from 1913 to 1921. His declaration of American neutrality at the outbreak of World War I was the subject of heated debate. Even Roosevelt was initially unsure about the best policy for America concerning the war in Europe.

However lofty its cause, the Progressive Party was at a distinct disadvantage. Despite Roosevelt's enormous personal popularity, the new party did not have strong local organizations. And at that time elections were won and lost at the local level.

The Progressives did manage to take support away from Taft. The incumbent President received only 8 electoral votes, Roosevelt got 88, and the winner, Democrat Woodrow Wilson, received 435. Wilson's platform was similar to that of the Progressive Party. But the Democrat was backed by strong local party organizations, and that had made a major difference.

Again Roosevelt retired from politics, this time to

The assassination of Archduke Franz Ferdinand and Princess Sophie of Austria in 1914 triggered the events which led to World War I. The United States entered the war in 1917, when the Wilson administration recognized that only American participation could end the conflict.

work on his autobiography. But the apostle of the strenuous life was still not ready to sit by the fire and dream of past glories.

After finishing the autobiography, he made plans for yet another scientific expedition. This one, to South America, would be sponsored by the American Museum of Natural History in New York. It was the museum his father had helped found, to which young Teedie had contributed his first scientific specimens. Roosevelt said about the trip, "I had to go. It was my last chance to be a boy." But it turned into a man-sized adventure.

In October 1913 Roosevelt and his wife set sail. In Brazil they were joined by Kermit, who had been working on bridge construction there. After a triumphant six-week speaking tour, Roosevelt and

The British liner *Lusitania* and the German submarine which sank her. Over 100 Americans died when the *Lusitania* went down on May 7, 1915, provoking Roosevelt to accuse the Germans of "murder on the high seas."

The New York Times.

EXTRA
5:30 A.M.

VOL. LXIV. NO. 20,921.   NEW YORK, SATURDAY, MAY 8, 1915.—TWENTY-FOUR PAGES.

LUSITANIA SUNK BY A SUBMARINE, PROBABLY 1,260 DEAD; TWICE TORPEDOED OFF IRISH COAST; SINKS IN 15 MINUTES; CAPT. TURNER SAVED, FROHMAN AND VANDERBILT MISSING; WASHINGTON BELIEVES THAT A GRAVE CRISIS IS AT HAND

SHOCKS THE PRESIDENT

Washington Deeply Stirred by the Loss of American Lives.

BULLETINS AT WHITE HOUSE

Wilson Reads Them Closely, but Is Silent on the Nation's Course.

HINTS OF CONGRESS CALL

Loss of Lusitania Recalls Firm Tone of Our First Warning to Germany.

CAPITAL FULL OF RUMORS

SOME DEAD TAKEN ASHORE

Several Hundred Survivors at Queenstown and Kinsale

STEWARD TELLS OF DISASTER

One Torpedo Crashes into the Doomed Liner's Bow, Another Into the Engine Room.

SHIP LISTS OVER TO PORT

ATTACKED IN BROAD DAY

The Lost Cunard Steamship Lusitania
X Where the First Torpedo Struck.   XX Where the Second Torpedo Struck.

Only 650 Were Saved, Few Cabin Passengers

Cunard Office Here Besieged for News; Fate of 1,918 on Lusitania Long in Doubt

List of Saved Includes Capt. Turner; Vanderbilt and Frohman Reported Lost

Saw the Submarine 100 Yards Off and Watched Torpedo as It Struck Ship

---

On May 8, 1915 *The New York Times* **announced the sinking of the** *Lusitania.* **In spite of the German act of aggression, President Wilson continued to keep America out of the war, prompting Roosevelt to call him "an abject coward."**

his party joined forces with a group led by Colonel Rondon, a famous Brazilian explorer. Together the two groups would explore an uncharted river, the Rio da Dúvida (River of Doubt).

On February 27, 1914, they entered the headwaters of the river. Very quickly the challenges surfaced. Canoes had to be carried through thick growth around the numerous waterfalls. Sometimes canoes were lost or damaged in dangerous rapids. One of the native paddlers drowned in the swift current, and Kermit himself barely escaped a similar fate. Hostile forest natives shot poisonous arrows at the intruders. Fever gripped many of the explorers, including Roosevelt and his son.

Through it all, the former president found time to keep up his journal. While others collapsed from the day's exertions, he sat at his portable desk. Head swathed in mosquito netting, hands encased in thick gloves, he worked on a series of magazine articles later published as the book *Through the Brazilian Wilderness.* At times he shook so from fever that the handwriting was barely legible. On one page he scribbled in the margin that his temperature was 105 degrees.

At one point, attempting to save a canoe from rapids, Roosevelt injured his leg. The wound became inflamed and developed abscesses. He was delirious with fever and lay deadly ill for 48 hours. When the fever subsided, he pleaded with Kermit to be left behind so that the others might push on and thus avoid starvation, which was a constant threat.

Of course, his request was refused. In the end, the unbelievable hardships were overcome, and the Roosevelt-Rondon party accomplished its goal. The group completely traced the course of a river nearly 1,000 miles long. It was only fitting that the river was renamed Rio Roosevelt.

The first American troops to arrive in France parade at St. Nazaire, June 1917.

By May 1914 Roosevelt was back in New York. He had lost at least 35 pounds and appeared much older. His face was more lined and his voice lacked its former power. He was to suffer from attacks of fever and a weakened constitution for the rest of his life. But as one reporter noted, "None of the old-time vivacity of manner was lacking."

On June 28, 1914, the assassination of the Austrian archduke in Sarajevo, Yugoslavia, precipitated the events that led to World War I. One by one the European nations were drawn into the conflict. The United States was officially neutral, and President Wilson was determined to keep it that way.

At first Roosevelt supported the President's position, but he soon became convinced that the United States should and would enter the conflict. In part his moral sense reared up at the injustice of some of Germany's actions. It is also likely that the old

America's Secretary of War Newton D. Baker greets American troops training in France during World War I. Roosevelt was desperate to command a division in France, but President Wilson refused to grant his request. World War I required professional soldiering, not, thought Wilson, the amateurism of a man like Roosevelt.

warrior sniffed another opportunity for heroic deeds.

Roosevelt began to attack Wilson's position on the war and to speak out for military preparedness. He stepped up his campaign when Germany announced that its submarines would attack unarmed ships flying the British flag. When the *Lusitania* was sunk by Germans in May 1915 and 128 American lives were lost, Roosevelt became even more enraged with Wilson's policy of neutrality.

In 1916 he rejected the Progressive Party's nomination for president and threw his support to Republican nominee Charles Evans Hughes. He was convinced that a third party could not win, and he wanted to do everything possible to assure Wilson's defeat. But Wilson was reelected with the slogan "He kept us out of war."

As the war in Europe dragged on, Roosevelt began to bombard President Wilson and Secretary of

War Baker with letters and visits. He sought permission to raise a fighting division should America enter the war. His requests were repeatedly turned down. Possibly Wilson was punishing his severest critic. Possibly he realized that the old Rough Rider was ill-prepared for the modern trench warfare being fought in Europe.

When the United States finally did declare war in April 1917, Roosevelt again requested permission to head a division. He even offered to raise the money to arm and train his men until Congress could pass a war appropriations bill. Again he was turned down.

Roosevelt's cause received the support of Georges Clemenceau, the former premier of France, who urged Wilson to send T.R. with an expeditionary force. He said it would be a symbol to the war-weary French that American help was on the way.

American troops march through the streets of Paris on July 4, 1917. French Premier Clemenceau begged President Wilson to send Roosevelt to France, claiming that his presence would boost morale. Wilson refused, feeling that Roosevelt's previous combat experience was no preparation for fighting in a modern war.

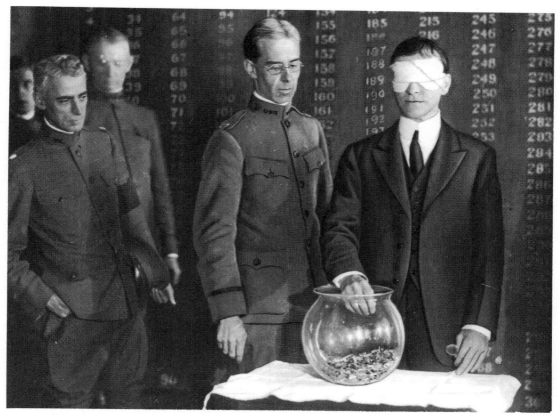

Secretary of War Newton D. Baker (blindfolded) draws the first number for the second military draft of World War I. Neither Baker nor President Wilson liked the prospect of war. Speaking of his official declaration of war on Germany, Wilson said, "My message was a message of death to our young men."

Still Wilson refused to send the frustrated Roosevelt.

Nevertheless, to the people of the world Roosevelt was still a symbol of America. Thus, when the American Expeditionary Force arrived in Paris on July 4, 1917, the French cheered, "Vive les Teddies."

The disgruntled Roosevelt had to stay at home and take pride in his children's service to their country. Even before the United States had declared war, his daughter Ethel and her husband had gone to France with the Red Cross. Now all four of his sons enlisted and were sent overseas.

Roosevelt himself was bitterly disappointed that he did not see action. His war effort was limited to making speeches supporting the war and at the same time criticizing Wilson's handling of it.

From Sagamore Hill he wrote loving letters of encouragement to his four sons overseas. In July

Lieutenant Quentin Roosevelt of the U.S. Army Air Service in France during World War I. Theodore Roosevelt was shattered by the news of Quentin's death in July 1918. The vehemence of his anti-German speeches increased, and he demanded that Germany's eventual surrender be unconditional.

Roosevelt is not an American, you know. He is America.
—JOHN MORLEY, writer

1918 he and Edith received word that their youngest son, Quentin, had been killed behind enemy lines. It was a severe blow to a man who loved his family above all else.

The war ended in November 1918, and already there was talk of drafting Roosevelt for president in the 1920 election. But the Bull Moose was beginning to show signs of weariness. The fever that he had first contracted in Cuba and that had almost killed him in South America continued to plague him. There were other signs that his body was not keeping up with his spirit.

On January 6, 1919, Theodore Roosevelt died in his sleep at Sagamore Hill. Vice-President Marshall commented, "Death had to take him sleeping, for if Roosevelt had been awake, there would have been a fight."

His son Archie cabled to Ted and Kermit, still on duty in Europe, "The old lion is dead." But while the lion had indeed laid down his body, his exuberant spirit lived on in the minds and hearts of people everywhere.

To those who knew him and to those who had only heard of him, Theodore Roosevelt became an enduring symbol. He was raw energy, unbounded enthusiasm, unquenchable confidence, iron determination. He was America at the turn of the century.

Mourners at Theodore Roosevelt's funeral, January 12, 1919.

Chronology

October 27, 1858	Born at 28 East 20th Street, New York City
1880	Graduated from Harvard
	Married Alice Hathaway Lee
1882-84	Member of the New York State Legislature
1884	Death of mother and wife
1884-86	Rancher in Dakota Bad Lands
1886	Republican candidate for mayor of New York City
	Married Edith Kermit Carow
1889-95	Member of U.S. Civil Service Commission
1895-97	President of New York City Board of Police Commissioners
1897-98	Assistant Secretary of the Navy
1898	Lieutenant Colonel and then Colonel of First Volunteer Cavalry (Rough Riders) in war against Spain
1899-1900	Governor of New York
1901	Vice-president of United States
1901-09	President of the United States
1906	Awarded Nobel Peace Prize
1909-10	Scientific safari to Africa; tour of Europe
1912	Presidential candidate of American Progressive Party
1913-14	Exploration of Brazil's Rio da Duvida (renamed Rio Roosevelt)
1914-17	Campaign for military preparedness
January 6, 1919	Died at Sagamore Hill in Oyster Bay, New York

Further Reading

Bishop, Joseph Bucklin, ed. *Theodore Roosevelt's Letters to His Children.* New York: Charles Scribner's Sons, 1947.

Eliot, John L. "T.R.'s Wilderness Legacy." *National Geographic,* Vol. 162, No. 3, September, 1982, pp. 340-63.

Gardner, Joseph L. *Departing Glory: Theodore Roosevelt as Ex-President.* New York: Charles Scribner's Sons, 1973.

Harbaugh, William H. *The Life and Times of Theodore Roosevelt.* New York: Oxford University Press, 1975.

Johnston, William Davison, *T.R., Champion of the Strenuous Life.* New York: Theodore Roosevelt Association, 1958.

McCullough, David. *Mornings on Horseback.* New York: Simon and Schuster, 1981.

Morris, Edmund. *The Rise of Theodore Roosevelt.* New York: Coward, McCann & Geoghegan, 1979.

Morris, Sylvia Jukes. *Edith Kermit Roosevelt.* New York: Coward, McCann & Geoghegan, 1980.

Mothner, Ira. *Man of Action: The Life of Theodore Roosevelt.* New York: Platt & Munk, 1966.

Pringle, Henry F. *Theodore Roosevelt.* New York: Harcourt, Brace & World, 1956.

Index

Lois Markham is a writer and editor specializing in educational materials. She has written frequently about television and is the editor of a series of books on writing. A former teacher, she lives in New York City, where she pursues her interests in natural history, dance, and literature.

Arthur M. Schlesinger, jr. taught history at Harvard for many years and is currently Albert Schweitzer Professor of the Humanities at City University of New York. He is the author of numerous highly praised works in American history and has twice been awarded the Pulizer Prize. He served in the White House as special assistant to Presidents Kennedy and Johnson.